ABOUT EDWIN SILBERSTANG

"The man many consider to be the greatest gaming authority in the world."
Len Miller, Editor-in-Chief, Gambling Times Magazine

"Ed Silberstang knows more about gaming from the inside and out than anyone writing on the subject today."
John Luckman, Gambler's Book Club

ABOUT THE AUTHOR

Edwin Silberstang is acknowledged by the top professionals in the gaming world as the leading authority on games in America. His first gaming book, Playboy's Book of Games, published in 1972, was an instant best-seller and a selection of the Book of the Month Club.

Since then, Silberstang has published over forty books dealing with games, gambling and the Vegas scene. His expertise has been used in the entertainment world, and he was the technical adviser on the film, Big Town, a story about a young gambler starring Matt Dillon, produced by Columbia Pictures.

In addition, he has written and starred in his own videos about gaming, and has appeared on many television and radio shows throughout the country. He is constantly called upon as a consultant and teacher as well.

Silberstang's success in the field comes from a skill as a novelist combined with a vast knowledge of gaming. His writing is clear and concise and he not only is able to present information but to make it interesting and fascinating.

HANDBOOK OF
WINNING
BRIDGE

HANDBOOK OF
WINNING
BRIDGE

Edwin Silberstang

CARDOZA PUBLISHING

To Les Lang

Cardoza Publishing, publisher of **Gambling Research Institute** (GRI) books, is the foremost gaming and gambling publisher in the world with a library of more than 50 up-to-date and easy-to-read books and strategies. These authoritative works are written by the top experts in their fields and with more than 5,000,000 books in print, represent the best-selling and most popular gaming books anywhere.

First Edition

Library of Congress Catalog Card No: 94-69972
ISBN: 0-940685-56-6

CARDOZA PUBLISHING
P.O. Box 1500, Cooper Station, New York, NY 10276
Phone (718)743-5229 • Fax (718) 743-8284

Write for your <u>free</u> catalogue of gaming books, advanced strategies and computer games.

TABLE OF CONTENTS

4. BIDDING STRATEGY 37

5. OPENER'S REBIDS 73

6. PRE-EMPTIVE OR SHUT-OUT BID 79

7. SLAM BIDDING 83

1. INTRODUCTION

Bridge is one of the most popular games invented by man and since its introduction in 1926, it has attracted millions of players. It is truly an international game and is played in every country of the world. There are a number of good reasons for its popularity. First of all, it is a partnership game, and this social aspect differentiates it from games in which an individual plays against other individuals, such as poker.

Also, unlike many other card games, it can be played for the pure enjoyment of the game. The game requires a great deal of skill combined with a little luck, and in some forms of bridge, such as duplicate where teams of four play against each other, it is a game of pure skill. With this emphasis on skill, there is no necessity for the game to be played for money.

If four bridge players get together, an enjoyable evening of cards can be arranged, with one partnership playing against the other. The partners can switch so that each player will play as partner with the other three participants. Or the partnerships can be fixed. When a partnership is set, the players can enter tournaments and win master points and titles. There is no end to the possibilities and pleasures of this great game.

The game is played mostly as rubber bridge. This is the home version of contract bridge, and our emphasis will be on this aspect of the game. But as one's skill increases, the same principles that were learned in rubber bridge can be applied to duplicate bridge, which is the format for tournaments. All this will be covered fully in this book.

For now, it is important to remember that the same principles of bidding and playing out of hands apply to both rubber and duplicate bridge. The basic difference is that when playing rubber bridge, one partnership or side plays against the other, attempting to win two games, or a rubber.

In duplicate bridge, a partnership will play individual hands against many other partnerships. The scoring is also different. When we discuss scoring, such as points scored, points needed for game and slam, penalty points, etc., it is always in the context of rubber bridge.

The game of bridge has two distinct parts, both of which must be mastered in order to play the game skillfully. The first part of the game is involved with bidding, in which the partners attempt to reach a contract that they can make. The second part is involved with the play of the hand. Both are of equal importance. In this book, we're going to take you step by step through each process, so that you'll be able to play the game at a competent and skillful level.

In addition to this, we're also going to show you how the game is scored, bidding conventions, finesses and all the other information that will enable you to understand and enjoy bridge to its fullest. It is a fascinating game, and players who have played all their lives still find something new each time the game is dealt. There are truly millions of possible hands that can come up in any deal, and the challenges of bridge are always fresh and new. Certainly this has contributed to its immense popularity.

What we're going to do in this book is teach you the game from the very beginning. For those who are somewhat familiar with the game, we'll review correct bidding and playing skills. Our aim is to make you a better player, so that you can enjoy this fascinating game to the utmost. No matter what level of skill you have at bridge, this book will make you a better player.

From the basics to the most popular bidding conventions, from the standard to the subtle plays involving the playing out of the hand, we'll show you how to play the game at its best level. We want to inspire you to play the game so that you realize the enjoyment that comes as a reward to those who do something well.

So, whether you will play bridge at home or will attempt to play in tournaments, by the time you finish this book, you'll be fully prepared to be a winner at bridge!

2. RULES OF PLAY

THE PARTNERSHIP

One of the unique qualities of bridge is the fact that it is a partnership game in which the partners, within certain limits, are able to signal the strength of their hands during the bidding as well as during the playing out of the hands.

Bridge is a game played by four players, forming two sets of partners-one partnership known as **East** and **West**, the other known as **North** and **South**. Any diagrammed bridge hand will follow that format, setting up the hands as follows:

N

W   E

S

As can be seen by the diagram, the partners sit opposite each other. The result of the play is shared equally by the partners, and one score is kept for each partnership. Thus, if East and West bid and make one club, the score would be twenty points for East-West, not twenty points for East and twenty points for West. Because of the partnership aspect of bridge, the partners must co-operate with each other during the bidding, and when defending the contract, during the playing out of the hands.

Bridge is basically an unselfish game, in which a player must sublimate his interests for the good of the partnership. If you play with this attitude, you'll be a good partner, and you'll add to the enjoyment of the game.

CARDS

The standard fifty-two deck is used, without the jokers. Generally, in the course of a game of rubber bridge, two decks are used, one being dealt and the other, usually with a different colored back, being shuffled in readiness for the next deal. The standard method is to have the dealer's partner shuffle the other deck and then place the deck to the right of the player between the dealer and shuffler - in other words, next to the player who will deal next.

RANKS OF THE CARDS

The standard deck that bridge is played with consists of four suits, Spades, Hearts, Diamonds and Clubs. Within each suit is thirteen cards. The ace is the highest ranking card, followed by the king, queen, jack, 10,9,8,7,6,5,4,3, with the 2, or deuce, being the lowest ranking of all the cards. In the course of this book, we may abbreviate the cards as follows: Ace = A, King = K, Queen = Q and Jack = J. The numbered cards will be shown by their numbers; ie. 8 = 8.

THE DEAL

The deal moves in a clockwise fashion, with each player holding the deal once each four games. If South was the first dealer, then West would deal next, followed by North and finally East.

Before dealing, the dealer gives the cards to the player

to his right to be cut, then he restacks the cards and proceeds to deal. If South is the dealer, the first card will be dealt to West, then a card to North, a card to East and finally a card to himself. The cards are dealt face down and all the cards are dealt out. Thus, at the end of the deal, each player will have thirteen cards.

While the cards are being dealt out, they shouldn't be picked up by the other players, till all the cards have been dealt out. If there's been a mistake in the deal,with one player getting too many or too few cards, this can be remedied as long as the cards haven't been seen by the players. Once they've been looked at, a mistake would result in a misdeal, with all hands dead. A new deal would then have to be made.

SORTING THE CARDS

After all the cards have been dealt out, the players pick up the cards and sort them by suits. Within the suits, cards are sorted by their relative rank, from highes to lowest. Bridge is a game in which the bidding and playing out of cards is by suits, and therefore, it is necessary to hold your cards by suits. A typical holding would look like this:

♠ A 10 8 5 ♥ 9 7 ♦ J 9 8 ♣ K Q 3 2

RANK OF SUITS

In contract bridge, the suits have a definite value both in bidding and scoring. The highest-ranking suit is spades, followed by hearts, diamonds and last of all, clubs. Spades and hearts are known as the **major suits**, while diamonds and clubs are the **minor suits**. When scoring, as we shall see, the major suits are accorded thirty points each, while the minor suits receive only twenty points.

Because of the different ranks of the suits, the bidding

follows a specific order. The lowest bid of any suit is in clubs. Next comes diamonds, followed by hearts, with the highest bid of a suit being spades. If suits are bid, a bid of one club can be followed by a bid of one diamond, one heart and then one spade. But if a bid of one spade is made, since it is the highest-ranking suit, the next bid will have to be at the two level. You cannot have a bid of one spade followed by a bid of one heart. The bidder of hearts would have to bid at least two hearts.

NO-TRUMPS

Bridge contracts can not only be made in the four suits, but also in No-Trump. **No-Trump** is just what the name implies. None of the suits is trump. As we shall see, when a final bid is made in the course of the bidding, that bid determines the trumps. For example, if the final bid was four spades, then spades would be trump. If the final bid was five clubs, then clubs would be trump. However, if the final bid is three No-Trump, then no suit would be trumps.

No-Trumps is the highest possible bid at any level. To refresh our recollection, the highest suit bid is spades. If a bid is one spade, a bid in No-Trump can also be made, since this is the highest possible bid at any level.

TRUMPS

One of the purposes of bidding is for a partnership to have the final say in what suit shall be trumps, or if the partnership so prefers, to play out the hand in No-Trump. When a particular suit is trumps, that suit is more powerful than any other suit during the playing out of the hand.

When a player is void in a suit, that is, has no more of a particular suit other than trumps, he can play a trumps to win the trick. We'll go into this in greater detail later, but for now, it's important to remember that trumps is the strongest of all suits when a hand is being played out.

For example, let's say diamonds are trumps, and an A of hearts was led, with another player playing the Q of hearts, followed by another player putting down the jack of hearts. If the fourth player was void in hearts, he could play the 2 of diamonds, which is trumps, and win the trick.

OBJECT OF THE GAME

The object of bridge is to bid for a particular contract and then win enough rounds of cards, known as **tricks**, to justify that bid. If a partnership bids and makes as many or more tricks than the bid called for, the partnership will be rewarded with points. If it fails to make the tricks needed to justify the bid, it is said to **go down**, or **be set,** and the other side is awarded points.

BASICS OF BIDDING

Contract bridge, as we have mentioned, is divided into two distinct parts. First there is the bidding, then the playing out of the hand. The purpose of bidding is to reach a contract that can be made for maximum scoring. The ideal contract gives the partnership bidding it the highest number of points based on the strengths of the two hands of the partnership. Sometimes we find that both partnerships have rather strong hands, and then the bidding becomes competitive, with each partnership trying to put in the final bid so that they can determine what suit will be trumps or whether they care to play the hand in No-Trumps.

The lowest possible bid is at the **one-level**, such as one heart. When this bid is made, what the bidder is saying in essence is that he has a strong enough hand to open the bidding, and if the bid ends at one heart, with all other players passing, he can make seven tricks by playing out the hand.

The reason he has to make seven tricks rather than just one trick, which he bid, is that the first six tricks are called *book*. It is assumed in bridge that all bids are added onto *book* to determine how many tricks a partnership must win to make the contract. A bid of three No-Trump means that nine tricks must be won. A bid of seven clubs means that all thirteen tricks must be won, without the loss of any tricks. When such a bid and contract is made, it is known as a **grand slam.**

Going back to the ranks of the suits, we can see that the lowest possible bid that can be made is one club. And the highest possible bid is seven-no-trump. However, suit and no-trump bids are not the only valid bids that can be made. A player may pass and not make any suit or no-trump bid. If a player passes, this doesn't foreclose him from coming back and making another bid of a suit, no-trump or double. A double is usually a bid made to penalize the opposing partnership when a player feels that they have bid the wrong suit or shouldn't have bid no-trump or have bid too high, so that they cannot win sufficient tricks to fulfill their contract.

A **trick** is a round of play in which each participant plays one card from his hand. Altogether there are thirteen tricks to be played and won.

There are other possible reasons for bidding a double, but we'll cover them in the appropriate sections. For now, we should know that a double is a valid bid open to the bidders. A player, after a double is bid by the opposing partnership, can redouble. A redouble means that the player redoubling feels the double bid was in error and that he can fulfill his contract.

So, now, let's review all the possible bids that can be

made in contract bridge. First, there's a suit bid, then a no-trump bid, a pass, double and redouble. Let's follow an imaginary session of bidding to see how these bids can be made. To start off, we'll look at our diagram of the four players involved in the bidding. The first player to bid is the dealer. The (D) next to South will indicate that he is the dealer, and thus the first to bid.

The sequence of bidding is always clockwise. In the diagram below it would start with South, then West, North and East would bid in order. The bidding ends when there are three consecutive passes after the last bid.

N

W E

S (D)

SOUTH	WEST	NORTH	EAST
One heart	Pass	One Spade	Two Clubs
Two spades	Pass	Four spades	Double
Pass	Pass	Redouble	Pass
Pass	Pass		

In the above bidding sequence South opened the bidding with a bid of One Heart, showing a fairly strong hand. If he had a weak hand, he could have passed. West who was next to bid, passed and continued to pass during the entire bidding sequence. It was his partner, East, who doubled the contract bid of four spades, and his double was answered by a redouble by North, the original bidder of spades. After the redouble, there were three passes, which ended the bidding. Anytime the bidding produces three passes after a bid of a suit, no-trump, double or re-double, the bidding ends.

If all the players have weak hands,and there are four passes on the opening round of bidding, the bidding ceases and all the players throw in their cards. The sequence would look like this:

WEST (D)	NORTH	EAST	SOUTH
Pass	Pass	Pass	Pass

A double or redouble keeps the bidding alive, and there may be more bids after that. The next sequence of bids will show this situation. North is the dealer.

NORTH (D)	EAST	SOUTH	WEST
Pass	One Diamond	One spade	Two Hearts
Three Clubs	Double	Redouble	Three Hearts
Pass	Pass	Pass	

After the redouble by South, West still had a chance to bid three hearts. The three subsequent passes ended the bidding.

TRICKS

We have mentioned the taking in of tricks, or the winning of tricks. A trick is a round where all four players play a card. The highest ranking card of the suit wins the trick, if all four players have that suit. For example, suppose South led the 9♣. By **led**, we mean that he was the first to play a card on a particular round. If West put down or played the

4♣, North the Q♣ and East the 5♣, then the trick is won by North, since the Queen is the highest ranking of the cards played on that round.

Altogether there are thirteen tricks to be won, one for every card the players hold. Each of the players must be aware of the potential for taking in tricks with the cards in their hand; especially the partners who bid a particular contract. By **contract**, we mean the result of the final bid, which determines just how many tricks the partnership must win to fulfill the contract. If the final bid is at the four level, such as four spades, then the partnership must win ten tricks to make or fulfill the contract. The partnership can win more than ten tricks; that is fine and enables them to get extra points in the scoring. But first and foremost, ten tricks must be won. The defenders, the other partnership, will endeavor to win at least five tricks to **set** or defeat the contract. By winning at least five tricks, points will be awarded to the defenders.

Therefore, when bidding, it is important to know just how many tricks can be won with both partners' cards. Special emphasis is placed on high ranking cards and trumps, which are important cards for taking in tricks. As we may recall, one of the goals of bidding is to name the suit that will be trumps. Whatever the final bid is in a suit, that suit automatically becomes trumps. Thus, if the final bid is two diamonds, diamonds is trumps. If the final bid is four hearts, hearts are trumps, and so forth. When the final bid is in no-trump, then no suit can be used as trumps; all suits are equally strong.

One of the powerful uses of trumps is when a player is void in a led suit. For example, if spades are trumps, and a player is void in clubs, if a club is led, he can play a trumps on it at his discretion, and win the trick, no matter what the rank of his trumps. If a 10, Queen and Ace of clubs were played, and the last player to put down a card is void in clubs, by playing any spades, which is trumps, he wins the trick. We mentioned that he may play a trumps at his discretion - when a player is void in a suit, he can play any other suit, but these will be losers. Only a trump will win the trick.

Let's follow this as an example. Spades are trumps. The 3 of diamonds is led, followed by the 7 and king of diamonds. The last player to play has no more diamonds - he is void in that suit. But he elects not to trump the suit with the spades he holds. Instead he plays a club. Since he didn't follow suit and didn't play a trump, he cannot win the trick. The trick is won instead by the highest ranking of the diamonds, the king.

BASICS OF PLAY

Let us assume the following sequence of bids:

SOUTH	WEST	NORTH	EAST
One spade	Pass	Two spades	Pass
Four spades	Pass	Pass	Pass

The bidding is now complete, since there were three passes after the bid of four spades by South. The contract is in four spades, and thus spades are trump. Since South first bid spades, he is the **declarer**, the one who plays out the hand for the successful bidders. West and East are now the defenders, hoping to win enough tricks to set the contract. The bidding having been completed, it is now time to play out the hands.

The first lead is always made by the player to the declarer's left. In contract bridge, the defenders always lead first, a big advantage. For all tricks thereafter, the winner of the previous trick has the next lead.

Therefore in this contract, West leads the first card. West will play a card and then North, South's partner, will put down all of his cards face up on the table, where they will remain face up for all to see throughout the playing of the thirteen tricks. North is called the **dummy.** He no longer participates in the game. Declarer now makes all the plays, including the cards in dummy's hand.

After West has played his first card, the declarer now selects a card from dummy's hand to play. Then East plays a card, and finally the declarer puts down the fourth card on that round of play. A trick has been played, and won by one or the other of the partnerships. Whoever won the trick now plays first, and then four more cards are played with the winner of the trick again playing first, till all thirteen tricks have been played out.

After thirteen tricks have been played, each side counts the winning tricks. To fulfill his contract, South would have to have won at least ten tricks. If he has, he makes his contract. If he won less than ten tricks, then he is said to be *set*, and is penalized, with West and East getting a score for setting the contract.

That hand having ended, it is now West's turn to deal, and he deals out the thirteen cards to each player, and bidding starts anew. At this point, having mentioned scores, we will examine the scoring in contract bridge.

3. SCORING - GAME AND RUBBER

SCORESHEET

At the end of each game, the score of that game is entered on a scoresheet, which looks like this:

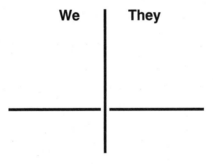

We | **They**

Usually, one of the partnerships keep score, and their score is **WE**. The score for the opposing partnership is set as **THEY**. The partnership is credited with the point score, not the individual players.

The horizontal line is an important separation of the scores. Only scores for tricks bid and made go below the horizontal line. All other scores, such as overtricks, penalties, honors, etc, go above the line. These scores will be fully explained later.

The only way a partnerhip can get points below the line is if they are the declaring side. The defenders cannot score below the line.

TRICK SCORES
Trick Scoring is as follows:

> • 20 points for each trick bid and made in diamonds or clubs.
> • 30 points for each trick bid and made in spades and hearts.
> • 40 points for the first trick bid and made in no-trump.
> • 30 points for each additional trick bid and made in no-trump.

Here are some examples, to make the scoring clearer.
• If you bid three clubs and won nine tricks, you'd score 60 points below the line.
• If you bid four spades and won ten tricks, then you'd score 120 points below the line.
• If you bid three no-trump and won nine tricks, then you'd score 100 points below the line.
• If you bid five diamonds and won eleven tricks, you'd score 100 points below the line.
• If you bid six no-trump and won twelve tricks, you'd score 190 points below the line.

GAME SCORE
The first partnership to reach 100 points wins **game**.

You may score game by winning one hand or by adding two or more hands together. In order to score game in one hand, you must bid and make the following:

Three no-trump	100 points
Four hearts or four spades	120 points
Five clubs or five diamonds	100 points

You can also win game by adding up the partial scores you have made. For example, if you bid and made two spades, you'd receive 60 points below the line. If, on the next hand you bid and made two clubs, that would be an additional 40 points below the line, giving you a total of 100 points, enough for game. The scoring would look like this:

We	They
60	
40	

It is also possible to have a partial score and then to have the opponents win game. For example, suppose you bid and made three hearts for 60 points. Then you bid and made one diamond for an additional 20 points. You'd now have 80 points. But suppose on the next hand your opponents, the other partnership, bid and made four spades for 120 points. They'd win game. The scoresheet would look like this:

We	They
60	120
20	

At this point, the game is finished. When all the points are eventually added up, you have 80 and the opponents have 120. But now another game must be played and a fresh scoresheet is started.

WINNING THE RUBBER

The first side or partnership to win two games wins the **rubber**. Winning the rubber is important because of all the bonus points attached. If you win the rubber two games to none, you score a bonus of 700 points. If you win the rubber two games to one, you score 500 bonus points. All rubber bonus points are scored above the line.

If you recall, we mentioned the term rubber bridge at the outset of the book. It gets its name from the rubber, which is the customary unit of play in contract bridge. After a rubber, partners may be changed if the players so desire, or another rubber will be played with the same partnerships.

UNFINISHED RUBBER

In the event that a rubber cannot be completed, the scoring is as follows:

UNFINISHED RUBBER	
One game won	300 points
Partial score	50 points

RUBBER POINTS

Winning the rubber - where opponents have won no game	700 points
Winning the rubber - where opponents have won one game	500 points
Unfinished rubber - winning one game	300 points
Unfinished rubber - for having only part score	50 points

VULNERABILITY

A side that has scored a game toward rubber is said to be **vulnerable**. If both sides have won a game, then both sides are vulnerable. A side that is vulnerable will be exposed to more severe penalties for failing to fulfill a contract. On the other hand, a vulnerable side will score higher bonus points in most cases than a side that is not vulnerable.

DOUBLED AND REDOUBLED TRICK POINTS

When you make a doubled contract, your trick score is doubled. You will receive the following points:
- 60 points for each trick bid and made in spades or hearts.
- 40 points for each trick bid and made in diamonds or clubs.
- 80 points for the first trick bid and made at no-trump.
- 60 points for any other trick bid and made at no-trump.

All of these points will be scored below the line and thus count toward game. For example, if you bid and make two spades doubled, your game score below the line is now 120 points instead of 60, the normal score for two spades bid and made. Bidding and making three clubs doubled will also give you game, since the 60 points for three clubs is now doubled to 120 points. However, bidding and making two diamonds doubled will not give you game; only 80 points or double 40 points.

When you bid and make a *redoubled* contract, then your score is quadrupled; that is, it's four times the normal value. Thus, if you bid and make one heart, which is ordinarily worth only 30 points, if it is doubled and re-doubled, it now is worth 120 points, good enough for a game score. Any bid in the two level, doubled and redoubled, is a possible game score. For example, two clubs, worth 40 points, now can count for 160 points, if the redoubled contract is made.

OVERTRICKS

Overtricks are tricks won by the declarer in excess of those necessary to make or fulfill the contract. For example, if the contract was four spades, which necessitates the winning of ten tricks, and the declarer made eleven tricks, he would have made one overtrick. If the contract was for two hearts, which called for the winning of eight tricks by the declarer and he made ten tricks, he would have made two overtricks.

The scoring for overtricks is the same as for bid and made tricks. The only difference is that overtricks do not count toward game and are scored above the line.

Let's assume that the first hand dealt called for a contract of three clubs. The declarer won eleven tricks, giving his side two overtricks, since he only needed nine tricks to fulfill his contract. It would be scored as follows:

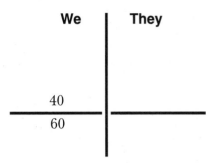

We	They
40	
60	

Although the declarer made 100 points in total, his side didn't win the game, since only the bid and made contract of three clubs goes below the line toward game score and the overtricks go above the line.

Above the line points, though not counting toward game or rubber, are important in their own right. At the end of a bridge session, all points on each side are added up to determine the winning partnership. For example, if one side won the rubber and scored 700 points above the line, plus another 240 points for game scores below the line, and the other side scored 1040 total points, the side with 1040 total points would beat the other partnership by 100 points.

In rubber bridge, all points are important, whether scored above or below the line. (See duplicate bridge section for duplicate bridge scoring.)

If the contract was doubled or redoubled, the following scores would be awarded, again, above the line. These scores are standard, no matter if the contract was played in a major or minor suit or no-trump.

OVERTRICKS (Doubled & Undoubled Contracts)

For each overtrick	Not Vulnerable	Vulnerable
Undoubled	Trick Value	Trick Value
Doubled	100	200
Redoubled	200	400

There is also a 50 point bonus for making a doubled or redoubled contract, whether or not the side was vulnerable or not vulnerable.

UNDERTRICKS

Each trick below the number of tricks necessary to make the contract is an **undertrick**. If the contract was for five clubs, and only eight tricks were made by the declarer, there would be three undertricks. Not making the contract penalizes the declarer's side, with the penalty points going to the other side, above the line.

The following are the penalty points:

UNDERTRICKS (Undoubled Contracts)

	Not Vulnerable	Vulnerable
First Undertrick	50	100
Each Additional Undertrick	50	100

UNDERTRICKS (Doubled Contracts)

	Not Vulnerable	Vulnerable
First Undertrick	100	200
2nd & 3rd Undertrick	200	300
Each Additional Undertrick	300	300

UNDERTRICKS (Redoubled Contracts)		
	Not Vulnerable	**Vulnerable**
First Undertrick	200	400
2nd & 3rd Undertrick	400	600
Each Additional Undertrick	600	600

HONORS

Certain high-ranking cards are known as **honors**. If a player holds all the honors, the Ace, King, Queen, Jack and 10 in the trump suit, or all four aces in no-trump, his side receives 150 points.

If a player holds any four of the honors in the trump suit, his side receives 100 points.

HONOR POINTS	
For holding in one hand:	
A K Q J 10 of trump	150 points
Four of the Five trump honors	100 points
All four aces in a no-trump contract	150 points

Any player may receive the honors bonus points, whether he is declarer, dummy or one of the defenders. The usual practice is to announce that you have held the honors at the *end* of play of the hand. This bonus is given whether or not the contract was made or set, or whether or not the side was vulnerable or not vulnerable.

SLAMS

There are bonuses given for bidding and making twelve tricks, **small slam**, or all thirteen tricks, the **grand slam**.

But note that the slams must be bid and made. If you bid four hearts and make all thirteen tricks, it is not a grand slam. The following are the bonus points for slams:

BONUS POINTS FOR SLAMS		
	Not Vulnerable	Vulnerable
Small slam	500	750
Grand slam	1000	1500

4. BIDDING STRATEGY

INTRODUCTION

Bidding allows the partners to exchange information, and also to glean information from the bids of the opposing partnership. Sometimes one side dominates the bidding on a particular hand, and nothing is learned from the other partnership, which will be the defenders. For example, in the following sequence:

SOUTH	WEST	NORTH	EAST
1 spade	Pass	2 spades	Pass
4 spades	Pass	Pass	Pass

All that the declaring side of South and North have learned from the bidding is that West and East are too weak to put in any kind of opening bid. All that the defenders have gleaned is that spades was bid, and nothing else. In this case, very little information passed between the partnerships.

We can now ask ourselves; what kind of hand is strong enough to bid on? How do we analyze our hands to open the bidding, and if our partner has bid, how do we respond?

These are important questions in bridge. We want to convey information about our hand to our partner, whether we open the bidding or respond to the partner's bid. Why do we want to do this? So that we can arrive at the correct contract, so that we can win the maximum number of points from our combined hands. To do this, we must know which suit to choose as trumps, or whether to play the hand in no-trumps instead of a suit trump.

The defenders also want to give information to each other during the bidding, but often they're precluded by the weakness of their hands from putting in any kind of bid. Since the defenders lead first, they must pay strict attention to the other side's bidding, to know which suit and card to lead.

The first step in correct bidding is to value our hand, for without knowing the true value of our hand, we will be playing a guessing game.

VALUING THE HAND

There are several methods to help us value our hands; the most important being the point count popularized by Charles Goren many decades ago. It is still valid and is the standard in contract bridge. It is based on the high cards in the hand, as well as the **short suits**, that is, suits holding two or one card, or no cards in a particular suit.

THE POINT COUNT

Practically all bridge players are familiar with this count, so, if you want to be able to play with any partner, you should know this count. Besides being popular, it is correct in evaluating and valuing a hand. First the high cards are given a value.

Each ace	4 points
Each king	3 points
Each queen	2 points
Each jack	1 point

Next we examine the short suits and their values.

Void suit - no cards in a suit	3 points
Singleton - one card in a suit	2 points
Doubleton - two cards in a suit	1 point

The above points are valid only for hands in which there is a suit trump. With no-trump hands, the short suit values aren't counted; just the high card points.

If we disregard the short suit or distribution points (the same thing) we can readily see that there are only 40 high card points in the entire deck.

Let's examine a few hands to see how many points we have:

♠ A Q J 5 3 ♥ K J 8 2 ♦ K 9 3 ♣ 5

We have 14 points in high cards and 2 in short suits (the club singleton) for a total of 16 points.

♠ K 8 4 ♥ J 9 6 ♦ A K Q 3 2 ♣ 9 4

We have 13 points in high cards and 1 in the short suit (the club doubleton) for a total of 14 points. If we were to evaluate the hand as a no-trump hand, it would contain just 13 high card points. Short suits do not help no-trump hands, as we shall see in the appropriate section.

Sometimes you cannot value a hand easily despite the point count. For example, if you have a singleton king; it is vulnerable to loss to an opponent's ace, and therefore cannot be given full evaluation as a high card.

It should be reduced from 3 to 2 points. As a singleton, it will still get two points as a short suit. Therefore, a valuation of 4 points for a singleton king would be in order. If you have a singleton queen, then it's high point value should be reduced from 2 to 1, with two points for the singleton as a short suit. The jack, however will yield no high card points as a singleton; it merely will get the 2 points as a short suited card. Aces are very important and powerful, since they command suits as the highest ranking card. Therefore a hand without an ace but with other high card points should be reduced by 1 point. Conversely, a hand containing three or four aces could be increased by one point.

POINTS NECESSARY FOR GAME

To refresh our recollection, game consists of four of a major bid and made (120 points), or five of a minor suit bid and made (100 points). In no-trump contracts, three no-trump has to be bid and made (100 points). Generally speaking, a total of 26 high and distributional points together in both partnership hands are necessary to bid and make a game in major suits. 29 points are necessary for game in the minor suits. In no-trump, only honor or high card points are counted.

If the parnership has less than these total points, it will usually have to settle for a partial score rather than a game score. For example, the partnership might have to settle on a contract of 3 spades or 4 diamonds, giving it a partial rather than a game score.

POINTS NECESSARY FOR SLAM

A small slam is six of any suit or no-trump bid and made. A grand slam is seven of any suit or no-trump bid and made.

---

33 points are necessary for a small slam.
37 points are necessary for a grand slam.

The above point totals don't guarantee that you can make the hand. It is a good guideline for game and slam bidding, but other factors may enter into the situation, such as how well your hand fits with your partner's hand, or the distribution of cards in a particular suit in a defender's hand. Sometimes you can reach game with only 24 or 25 points, if everything fits, but don't reach too far with too few points. That's the way to invite disaster; contracts that are set.

Let us now examine the factors that will determine whether or not we will make an opening bid.

OPENING SUIT BIDS AT THE ONE LEVEL

We should first explain what an **opening bid** is. It is the first bid made in a suit or no-trump. If West was the dealer and passed, then North passed and East bid one spade, that would be the opening bid. A pass is not considered an opening bid. There are several considerations that must be examined to determine whether or not we can open the bidding in a suit at the one-level; that is, bid either one club, one diamond, one heart or one spade.

BIDDABLE SUITS

The general rule is that any five-card or longer suit is biddable. In modern practice many players will need five cards in a major suit to bid at the one-level though some players might still bid a four-card major suit. The reason that five-card suits are preferable has to do with the rebidding by the opening bidder. A rebiddable suit is one which may be bid a second time. A four-card suit is not rebiddable in most cases, and since players prefer to play out hands in major suits because of the difference in scoring, it may be difficult to reach the correct contract if one opens a four-card major suit.

The exception is when you open a four-card major suit, such as spades, and your partner responds in spades, showing strength in the same suit. Then the four-card major may be rebid. But if the response is in a minor suit, the opener may be in a quandary, unless he has strength in another major suit. Let's look at a hand to illustrate this. You hold the following:

♠ A K 6 4   ♥ A Q 9 5   ♦ 8 7   ♣ 9 4 3

The hand contains 13 high card points and an additional point for the doubleton in diamonds, for a total of 14 points. You open with one spade and your partner responds with two diamonds. You can now bid your heart suit, giving your partner the choice of rebidding spades. If your partner had responded to your one spade bid with a bid of two hearts, then you know that hearts is the best suit for trump and you can raise to three hearts, and play out the hand at that contract.

We said that five card suits can be bid as opening one-level suit bids. We should also add that any five-card suit must be headed by at least a ten, while a four-card suit that is opened should have at least a Q J (or stronger cards) heading it. A king and 10 heading a four-card suit is acceptable. Thus, the following suits are biddable:

$$\clubsuit K\ 10\ 8\ 7 \qquad \clubsuit J\ 9\ 5\ 4\ 2$$

Let's now examine some major suits:

♠ A 10 9 5 4	This is a biddable suit
♥ J 7 5 2	This suit cannot be bid. It is a weak four-card major headed only by a jack.

POINT REQUIREMENTS FOR OPENING ONE IN A SUIT

In order to open the bidding at the one-level in a suit, you should have at least 13 points. But sometimes, even with 13 points (honor plus distributional points) it is difficult to find an opening bid because you have no biddable suit. Let's look at this situation in the following hand:

$$\spadesuit 10\ 9\ 5\ 4 \quad \heartsuit A\ Q\ 2 \quad \diamondsuit A\ Q\ 4 \quad \clubsuit J\ 8\ 6$$

Although we have a hand containing 13 honor points, there is no good opening bid. The spade suit has no honors and is only a weak four-card suit. The other suits have only three cards. However, if we redistribute these cards and change the structure of the suits, we come up with a correct opening bid.

$$\spadesuit 9\ 4 \quad \heartsuit A\ Q\ 10\ 5\ 2 \quad \diamondsuit A\ Q\ 4 \quad \clubsuit J\ 8\ 6$$

Now we can open with one heart. We have a five-card major suit headed by A Q, with the same 13 honor points, plus one additional point for distribution (the spade doubleton), making a total of 14 points.

Let's once again redistribute the cards and change the structure of the suits.

♠ 9 5 4 ♥ A Q 6 ♦ A Q 10 4 ♣ J 8 6

The major suits, spades and hearts, cannot be bid, since we only have three of each suit. However, our diamond suit is now of sufficient length, holding four cards, to make an opening bid of one diamond. With a minor suit, only four cards are necessary for an opening bid in a suit, provided that it is headed by sufficient honors, as in this case. We have 13 points in high cards, and a biddable diamond suit.

With 14 points in honors and in distributional points, we must make an opening bid. Bridge is a competitive game and we want to get an opening bid in, if possible, so that we are in charge of the bidding, rather than having the opponents get control. Then they're in charge of the bidding. Thus, with a biddable suit and 13 points we should bid in the one-suit level. With 14 points, we absolutely must make that first opening bid.

Let's look at another hand:

♠ 6 ♥ A 10 5 ♦ K Q 9 3 2 ♣ K 9 7 5

The above hand contains 12 points in honors, plus two distributional points for the spade singleton, for a total of 14 points. The heart suit contains only three cards and is not biddable. However, the diamond suit stands out with five cards headed by two honors. The logical bid here is one diamond.

Opening bids may be made with hands containing 12 points, if the bid suit is fairly strong, having two honors and a length of five or six cards. A good time to bid a hand weaker than 13 points is in third position, where an opening bid might disrupt the opposing player's potential opening bid. For example, if you hold 12 points and there have been two passes to you, you can venture an opening bid, if you have a biddable suit and only 12 points.

If your hand holds less than 12 points in distribution and high card points, don't open the bidding. Even if you are in the fourth seat and there have been three passes to you, you're only asking for trouble and a penalty if you open the bidding with a hand containing 10 or 11 points. Your partner has already passed, telling you he has a weak hand.

SHORT-CLUB BID

If you and your partner decide to bid only five-card major suits, the short-club convention is a good choice for an opening bid. It is an artificial bid, that is, the bid doesn't show strength in the suit bid, but is made for convenience. Here's how it works. Suppose you hold the following cards:

♠ K Q 8 3   ♥ A 9 7 2   ♦ A J   ♣ 8 7 5

There are 14 points in high cards, and therefore you want to make an opening suit bid. However, both your major suits are only four cards in length, and you bid only five-card majors. What do you do? If you and your partner have agreed on the short-club convention, you open with one club.

You now wait for your partner's response. You are telling him that you hold no five-card major biddable suit. If he responds with one of the major suits, then you know that will be the correct suit for the contract.

In essence, when you open the bidding at the one-suit level, you are beginning a dialogue with your partner. Between his responses and your rebids, you are attempting to find the correct contract. A correct contract is the highest possible bid that can be made. For example, if you and your partner arrive at a final contract of three spades, which is scored as 90 points, but in the course of play you won ten tricks, enough for four spades, then your bidding was incorrect. Instead of reaching game with 120 points, you only received 90 points below the line and 30 above the line for the overtrick.

If your final bid was four spades but you only were able to win nine tricks, and were set in the contract, going down one trick, again the bidding was wrong. What you must endeavor to do is bid a final contract that you will make with the exact number of tricks. This is easier said than done, of course, and sometimes, failing to make a contract will not be your fault. The distribution of trump cards in the opponent's hands might be uneven. Suppose as declarer you hold five spades and the dummy shows three, for a total of eight. Ideally, as we shall see in the section on playing out of the hand, you want the remaining trump to be split 3-2 among the other side. If it is split at 5-0, it is a bad break for you and may jeopardize the making of your contract. These things happen. Bridge is a game of skill, but luck does enter into it.

RESPONSES TO OPENING SUIT BIDS OF ONE

Up to this point, we've assumed you were the opener. But now, sitting at the bridge table opposite your partner, you find that she has opened the bidding with a one-suit bid. At this point, you are the **responder**. Your response is important, for it will show your partner the strength of your hand, and in what suits you have that strength. Thus, your partner, who opened the bidding, will be able to re-bid correctly, and you're on your way to finding the ideal and correct contract in which to play the hand. Being the responder, after the opening bid of one in a suit, you have several options open to you. We'll assume that the intervening player has passed, so that after your partner's first bid, your response will now be the next bid. Here are your options:

Unless you have at least six points in high cards in your hand, you should pass. There's a good reason for this rule. With less than six points in your hand, you have a very weak hand, and you won't be able to help out your partner. No matter how tempted you are to throw in a bid, a pass is in order, and in the long run, will save your from disastrous contracts and penalty points awarded to your opponents.

The following is a typically weak hand:

♠ J 6 3 ♥ 8 4 3 2 ♦ K 6 2 ♣ J 8 4

You only have five high card points, with no long suit and no doubleton or singleton, which would be of use to your partner. Pass.

A Raise of One over One -

A raise of **one over one** means a response at the same level as the opening bid in a suit. For example, suppose your partner bid one diamond. By bidding one heart or one spade, you're still staying in the same one-level. (A response of one-no trump will be dealt with in a later section; it is a special response.)

Suppose your partner opened with one heart and you

responded with two clubs. That is no longer a one over one response. Two clubs is in the two level. If you had responded instead with one spade, it would still be a one over one response.

This diagram shows a one over one response. You are North; your partner is South.

SOUTH	WEST	NORTH	EAST
1 Diamond	Pass	1 Spade	

Your response of one spade is a typical one over one bid.

A one over one response is not a weak bid; rather it is a **forcing bid**. By forcing, we mean that it strategically forces the opener to bid again for at least one more round in order to ensure that the partnership arrives at the best contract.

When we refer to *forcing*, it is always in the strategic sense, not as a law at bridge itself. Therefore, after responding one over one, you should expect your partner to rebid her hand.

However, if there is an intervening bid by an opponent, the opener is no longer required, or forced to bid again. Here is an example of an intervening bid by the other side.

Again, you and your partner are sitting North and South, with your partner, the dealer, making the first bid.

SOUTH	WEST	NORTH	EAST
1 Diamond	Pass	1 Spade	2 Hearts

East's bid of two hearts is an intervening bid, and now South is no longer forced to rebid. This is not to say that she is foreclosed from bidding, for she may certainly bid again depending on the strength of her hand, but she no longer is forced to make a rebid.

Requirements for Responding One Over One -

Your partner has opened with a suit bid at the one level. The following requirements are necessary for your response of one over one.

• Four or more cards in the bid suit.

• 6 to 17 points.

When making a response bid of one over one, the four card suit bid doesn't have to headed by an honor. All the responder needs is a four-card suit. Let's examine the next hand. You are holding these cards.

♠ K 6   ♥ 10 9 8 4   ♦ Q J 7   ♣ J 9 8 5

Your partner has opened with one diamond. You are holding 7 points in high cards and two four-card suits. By responding in hearts, you are keeping the bidding at the one-level and also responding in a major suit. When faced with a choice of a major suit or minor suit response with a hand like this, the major suit is always preferable. Suppose that instead of clubs, your other four card suit was spades, and thus, you have a choice of responding in either major suit. Respond in the lower of the two, hearts, in this situation.

The One No-Trump Response -

This response is often used just to keep the bidding open. Suppose you want to keep the bidding alive, but find that you have no suit that you can bid at the one-level, for a one over one response. And you also find that you have 6 or more honor points in your hand. You should think about a one no-trump response. Here's what you need to respond at one no-trump.

- 6 to 10 honor points. With a no-trump response, distributional points are not counted.
- No biddable suit at the one level.

Let's now look at some hands to see how this bid works.

♠ J 9 4　♥ 7 4　♦ Q 9 6 2　♣ A J 6 5

Your partner has opened with one heart. You have no biddable suit at the one-level. You have only three spades, and a diamond or club bid moves you into the second level of bidding. You have eight high points, and can't afford to pass. You want to keep the bidding alive. A one no-trump bid is therefore called for. Here's another hand:

♠ K 6　♥ 4 3　♦ A 8 6 3 2　♣ J 8 5 4

Again, your partner has opened with one heart. You have 8 honor points and cannot bid a suit in the one-level. A one no-trump response will keep the bidding alive.

In the next instance, your partner has opened with one spade, and you hold the following hand:

♠ 9 5 4　♥ K 9 5 2　♦ Q 10 8　♣ J 5 3

You have eight high points and want to keep the bidding alive; bid one no-trump.

Remember, with a one no-trump response, you are being very specific in limiting the honor strength of your hand. It will contain not less than six points and no more than ten points.

The response of one no-trump is not forcing, since the opener can ascertain the outer limits of his honor strength. If he has 13 points in his hand, he now knows that the most the partnership will have is 23 points, and possibly only 19, certainly not enough for game. To refresh our recollection, 26 points are needed for game.

Single Raise of Opener's Suit -

This is also a non-forcing bid, which means that the opener need not rebid his hand. A single raise is just what the name implies, a bid one higher than the opening bid in the same suit. For example, if the opening bid was one diamond, a two diamond response would be a single raise. Likewise a response of two hearts to a one heart opening bid.

Like the one no-trump response to an opening bid, a single raise is very specific in its limits. The following is necessary for a single raise in opener's bid suit:

- 7-10 points
- A minimum of three cards in the suit, if the opener bid a major suit, or four in the suit if a minor suit was opened.

Since most players open with a five-card major, the single raise will then assure the opener that the partnership has a fit of at least eight trumps. However, if a minor suit had been opened, it may have been opened with only four or even three cards by the original bidder, who will then know that the responder has at least four more trumps in his hand in the minor suit.

Note that the 7-10 points required for a single raise can come from both honor points and distributional values, unlike the one no-trump response, which required at least six honor points.

Let's now look at some representative hands. Your partner has opened with one spade and you hold the following hand:

♠ K 9 5 4   ♥ 9 5   ♦ J 7 6 2   ♣ Q 8 3

Respond with two spades. You have good trump support and 7 points - six in honors and one for the heart singleton.

In the next hand, your partner has opened with one heart and you hold the following:

♠ Q 8   ♥ 9 6 2   ♦ 10 8 5 3   ♣ Q 8 7 5

Your correct bid is to pass. You have only four honor points plus an extra point for the spade doubleton, two below the seven required for the single raise. Your hand is quite weak, with little support for your partner.

Let's look at one final hand. Your partner has opened one heart and you hold the following cards:

♠ 5 4   ♥ Q 9 3   ♦ A 9 5 2   ♣ 9 7 6 3

Your correct bid is two hearts, but it is a minimum raise with six honor points plus a point for the doubleton spade, and only three hearts.

One final note - remember that the single raise should not be made with more than ten points - it is limited to a range of 7-10 points, and is not forcing.

Two Over One Response -

This response occurs when you name a new suit at the two-level. The suit you are bidding is lower ranking than the suit your partner has opened with. For example, suppose your partner opened the bidding with one heart. If you had a good spade suit and the requisite points, you could still stay in the one-level with a response of one spades, a one over one response. Therefore, when you bid two over one, you cannot answer two spades to your partner's one heart bid, unless you have a great deal of power in your hand. This would be known as a **jump response**.

Let's go back to your partner's bid of one heart. To make a two over one response, you would have to bid one of the minor suits at the two-level. If your partner had opened with one spade, a two-bid in either of the remaining suits would be a two over one response. By remaining suits, we mean clubs, diamonds or hearts.

A response of two over one is forcing for one round. This means that your partner must rebid his hand; he is strategically forced to by your response.

Let's examine the requirements for a two over one response.
- A good suit, with five or more cards.
- At least 10 points in honors.
- 10-18 points, counting distributional strength.

Suppose your partner opened with one spade. You hold the following cards:

♠ 8 6 4   ♥ A 5   ♦ K Q J 9 3   ♣ 8 5 2

You hold 10 honor points, and an additional point for the doubleton hearts. You also have a solid five-card suit in diamonds. Your correct bid would be two diamonds, a two over one response. Let's examine some other hands:

You hold the following, and your partner has opened with one heart.

♠ 8 5   ♥ 3 2   ♦ J 5 4 3   ♣ A K Q 8 4

Bid two clubs. You have ten honor points and with two doubletons, a total of twelve points. You also have a strong five-card club suit.

Generally speaking, the two over one response is treated by experts as a decisive step towards a game contract. Let's go back to a previous hand to see how this may be done.

♠ 8 6 4   ♥ A 5   ♦ K Q J 9 3   ♣ 8 5 2

Your partner opened with one spade, and you correctly responded with two diamonds. Now you can bid further. Let's assume that your partner now rebid her spades, bidding two spades. You can raise to three spades, for the ideal contract seems to lie in spades. Between you, you have at least eight spades trump, assuming your partner opened with a five-card major.

In the next example, your partner has opened with one heart. You hold the following hand.

♠ 9   ♥ 9 6 5 3   ♦ A K Q 5 4   ♣ Q 8 2

Your correct response here is two diamonds. If your partner rebids his hearts you can raise in hearts, showing support with your four-card suit.

NO-TRUMP RESPONSES

So far, we've examined only the one no-trump response to an opening bid of one in a suit. To refresh our recollection, a one no-trump response showed 6-10 honor points (distributional points aren't counted in no-trump responses) and no biddable suit at the one level. Basically, a one no-trump response to an opening bid of one in a suit is a weak bid.

Requirements for other no-trump responses:

Two no-trump response shows the following:
• 13-15 points in high cards.
• Strength in each of the unbid suits. (If partner had opened with one heart, this means you will have strength in clubs, diamonds and spades).
• Balanced distribution. In no-trump contracts, short suits are detrimental to the playing out of the hand. They easily are depleted during the playing of the hand, and opponents may then run out the rest of the suit as winners. Since there are no trumps available, once you're void in a suit, the opponents have control if they lead that suit. Therefore, when we speak of balanced distribution, we don't want to see a singleton or a void suit.

Let's now look at a couple of hands. Your partner has opened with one heart and you hold the following hand:

♠ K J 5   ♥ 8 3   ♦ A Q 8 3   ♣ K J 7 6

You should bid two no-trump. Your hand holds 14 points in high cards (honors) and you have strength in all the suits except hearts, which was bid by your partner. Also your distribution, though not perfect, is balanced. You have a 3-2-4-4 distribution of suits. An ideal distribution for no-trump contracts is a 4-3-3-3 holding.

Another hand. Your partner has opened with one spade. You hold the following cards:

♠ 9 4   ♥ Q 10 6   ♦ A Q 8 5   ♣ K Q 9 3

Bid two no-trump. Your hand holds 13 high points, with strength in all the unbid suits, and a balanced distribution.

Three no-trump response shows the following:
  • 16-17 points in high cards.
  • Strength in each of the unbid suits.
  • Balanced distribution, preferably a distribution of 4-3-3-3.

The following hand should be bid at three no-trump following partner's opening bid of one spade:

♠ J 7 5   ♥ K Q 6   ♦ K Q 5   ♣ K Q 8 5

The above hand contains 16 high card points, strength in all the unbid suits, and a perfect 3-3-3-4 distribution.

JUMP RAISES BY RESPONDER

This is a strong response, promising a hand that is fairly powerful. A **jump raise** is one that is a level above the possible response. For example, if the opening bid was one spade, a jump raise would be three spades, jumping over the possible two spade response. When this occurs, it is called a jump raise in opener's bid suit (spade-spade). When the jump response to a one heart opening bid, for example, is two spades, this is known as a jump response in a new suit. This kind of jump response is more powerful than simply jump raising in opener's suit. Jump response in opener's suit:

The requirements are as follows:
- 13-16 points.
- At least four of the trump suit (suit bid), headed by at least a queen.

As you may recall, 26 points are needed for game, and since the opener is presumed to have at least 13 points, the jump response is telling the opener that game is possible, and it is considered as a bid forcing to game. The more trumps you hold, the higher you can bid, especially in a major suit.

MAJOR SUIT RAISES

When your partner opens the bidding with one in a major suit, you can raise her in that bid suit if you have sufficient trump support and enough card strength. The following table shows the points you need (high cards plus distributional points) as well as minimum trump strength.

MAJOR SUIT RAISES

- **Raise from 1 to 2.** (Example: Opener has bid one spade and you respond with a bid of two spades.) 7-10 points and three or four trumps (spades in this instance.) It is preferable, if holding three trumps, to have it led by at least a queen.
- **Raise from 1 to 3.** You need 13-16 points and a four card trump holding, headed by at least a queen.
- **Raise from 1 to 4.** Only 7-10 points are needed, but you must have five of the bid suit.

As mentioned before, the higher you raise, the more trumps you must have. When you bid four, you stop the bidding, telling partner in essence, "end the bidding; play the hand in four spades." A raise to four in the suit is known as a **shutout bid**. It stops the bidding by this partnership. With a bid of three spades, you're keeping the bidding alive. The above rules may seem a little complicated at first, but with experience at the bridge table, they'll become clearer. What is important is to arrive at a bid that best reflects the partnership's hands, and is the highest bid possible, because the higher the bid, the more points are scored. This is especially true at duplicate bridge, where your partnership is playing against many other partnerships, and each hand must be bid and made to the fullest limit to score winning points.

JUMP RESPONSE IN A NEW SUIT

A jump response is not only forcing to game, but carries with it the suggestion that the bidding might go all the way to slam. The following are the requirements for a jump response in a new suit:

- 19 points or more, both in high cards and in distributional values.
- A solid suit, or good support for opener's bid suit.

Let's examine some hands now. In the first example your partner has opened with one diamond. You hold:

♠ K 8   ♥ A K J 9 6   ♦ K Q 8 6   ♣ K 10

Your correct bid in this instance is two hearts. By making a jump response in a new suit, you're promising your partner at least 19 points, which you have in high cards alone. After your partner re-bids, you can show your support in his diamond suit.

Your partner in the next example has opened with one heart. You hold the following cards:

♠ A Q J 8 4   ♥ K Q 9 6   ♦ 7   ♣ K Q 3

Bid two spades here. Your jump response in a new suit shows that you have 19 points. When you rebid your heart suit, you will tell your partner that you also have strong support for his heart suit.

Thus far we've dealt with opening bids of one in a suit and the various responses to that bid. Now we'll switch to opening bids of one no-trump.

OPENING NO-TRUMP BIDS

The One No-Trump Opening Bid

No-trump is the fastest way to game in rubber bridge. It only takes nine tricks (three no-trump bid and made) for game, whereas it takes ten tricks bid and made in the major suits and eleven tricks bid and made in the minor suits. Just because it's the fastest way to game doesn't mean that you must take short-cuts and switch to no-trump whenever you feel like it. No-trump contracts require certain high card strengths and balanced distribution. Overlook these two factors and you and your partner are headed for trouble.

The following shows the necessary high card points for various contracts in no-trump.
- 26 points will usually be sufficient for a three no-trump game.
- 33 points will usually be sufficient for a six no-trump game.
- 37 points will usually be sufficient for a seven no-trump game.

Keep the above numbers in mind when bidding on a no-trump contract.

The following are the requirements for opening bids of one in no-trump:
  • 16-18 high card points. Distributional points do not count in no-trump contracts.
  • Balanced distribution. The following are considered balanced distribution in suits.

4-3-3-3 (the best)
4-4-3-2
5-3-3-2

  • All suits should be stopped. That is, there should be at least one honor covering each suit. The following are examples of protected and stopped suits. (x = small or indifferent card such as 8,6 or 2).

A x   K x   Q x x   J x x x

The ace, even as a singleton, will win a trick and stop a suit. The king needs another card with it for protection. The queen needs two other cards and the Jack three other cards to be able to stop a suit.

Here are some things to keep in mind when bidding no-trump contracts.

a. Your short suit is usually your opponent's long suit. You must guard against the possibility of an opponent establishing his long suit and cashing in tricks (winning tricks).

b. Avoid bidding no-trump contracts when you have a void or a singleton. Glance back now at the necessary distribution outlined above.

c. It is necessary to protect suits with stoppers. A stopper is any card that can prevent the opponents from running a suit (cashing in a number of tricks). The ideal stopper is the ace. Since the game is played without trumps, the ace is a sure winner of a trick. Another sure stopper would be the K-Q of a suit. Even if one falls to an opponent's ace, the other honor will win a trick. A king with a small card may be a stopper.

The same holds true for a queen and two small cards or a jack with three small cards. You can use them in bidding no-trump contracts, for they are all probable stoppers. Stronger than a queen with two small cards is queen-jack in a suit. Also strong is jack-10-9-8 of a suit. Therefore, if you have no probable stopper in one suit, avoid bidding no-trump.

d. Don't fudge on the high card point count. Don't stretch one no-trump opening bids with less than 16 points. Your partner should expect, when you open one no-trump, that you have 16-18 points, period!

We now know that 16-18 points is necessary for a one no-trump bid. As we shall see 22-24 points will be necessary to open at two no-trump. What about 19-21 high card points with balanced distribution?

Note: With 19-21 high card points and balanced distribution, open with one of a suit, and make a jump bid in no-trump after partner responds.

The following is necessary for an opening bid of two no-trump
- 22-24 high card points.
- Balanced distribution.
- All four suits must be protected; headed by honors. Unlike other opening bids in the two-level, which will be discussed later, a two no-trump opening bid is not

forcing. If the opener's partner has nothing, she may pass.

The following are the requirements for an opening bid of three no-trump.
- 25-27 high points.
- Balanced distribution.
- All four suits must be protected.

Let's examine some hands to see what the correct bid should be. You are dealt the following:

♠ A 5 4 ♥ K 9 3 ♦ Q J 10 ♣ A K J 5

You have 18 high card points and balanced distribution. There are stoppers in all suits. Bid one no-trump.

♠ K Q 9 ♥ A K J ♦ K Q 8 3 ♣ A J 6

You have 23 points in high cards, balanced distribution and stoppers in all suits. Bid two no-trump.

♠ K Q 8 ♥ A K J ♦ A K J ♣ K Q J 5

This hand contains 27 high card points, stoppers in every suit, perfect distribution of 3-3-3-4. Open the bidding with three no-trump.

RESPONSES TO OPENING NO-TRUMP BIDS

Whenever your partner opens the bidding in no-trump, you know the parameters of his bid in high card points. If he opened with one no-trump, you are aware that he holds 16-18 points. With an opening bid of two no-trump, he has 22-24 points and with a three no-trump opening bid, he is holding 25-27 points in high cards or honors. Therefore, it is much easier to know the strength of an opener bidding in no-trump than in a suit because the boundaries of his high card strength are more apparent. Let's first examine one no-trump opening bids.

Responses to Opening Bids of One No-Trump -
You must not lose track of the 26 points necessary to make game at three no-trump. Also, you must examine your hand to see if it is balanced or unbalanced as to distribution. A balanced hand could be one in which the distribution is 5-3-3-2, with the five card suit a minor suit. Of course, as we know, other distribution for no-trump could be 4-3-3-3 or 4-4-3-2.

• If you hold 0-7 points, you are interested in a part score (below 100 points).

• If you hold 8-9 points, you are also interested in a part score.

• If you hold 10 to 14 points, you want a game score (three no-trump).

• With 15 or 16 points, you are thinking of a possible slam.

• With 17 or more points, you are going to bid for a slam.

Remember, you need 26 points for game, 33 points for a small slam (6 no-trump) and 37 points for a grand slam (7 no-trump). When we discuss points, we are talking about high card points; distributional points play no role in no-trump bidding.

Knowing all this, here's what we do with our point totals:

• 0-7 points. We pass. We satisfy ourselves with a part score. Why? Because 7 and partner's 18 points (at best, he may be holding 16 points) don't add up to game.

• 8-9 points. We raise to two no-trump.

- 10-14 points. We raise to three no-trump.
- 15-16 points. We raise to four no-trump.
- 17-18 points. We raise to six no-trump, a small slam bid.
- 19-20 points. We think of a grand slam. Some ex perts advise not directly bidding six no-trump here, but first making a jump shift to three in a suit, then following up with a bid of six no-trump. They consider it stronger than just bidding six no-trump.
- 21 or more points. Bid the grand slam of 7 no-trump. Even if your partner has only 16 points, you're assured of at least 37 points. Since there are only 40 high points in the deck, and an ace is worth 4 honor points, your opponents aren't holding an ace when your partner ship has a combined 37 points.

THE STAYMAN CONVENTION

Popularized by Samuel Stayman, this convention is accepted worldwide by bridge players. In a nutshell, the **Stayman Convention** calls for a response of two clubs to a one no-trump opener, asking the opener to bid a four-card major. If the opener doesn't have a four-card major, the automatic rebid is two diamonds. Both the two club and two diamond bids are artificial, that is, they don't show strength in those minor suits, when bid in the Stayman.

Suppose the original bidder of one no-trump holds a four-card major. Then his reply will be in that major suit.

Here's how it would look diagrammed. South is the dealer and bidder of one no-trump; North is his partner.

SOUTH	WEST	NORTH	EAST
1 No-Trump	Pass	2 Clubs	Pass
2 Hearts			

By bidding two clubs, North is using the Stayman; and South's rebid of two hearts is telling his partner that he has a four-card major in hearts. Suppose that South has two four-card majors. He would then bid the spades first; and later bid the heart suit.

When the responder has used Stayman to find out if the opening bidder has a four-card major, and he is met with a rebid of two diamonds, denying any four-card holding in hearts or spades, he should not bid his own four-card major. In order to bid a major, he should have a five-card holding in that suit. If he holds only two four-card majors, he should return to no-trump, bidding two no-trump.

When you are the responder, and bid two clubs, and received a rebid of two diamonds, denying a four-card major, you now should go back to partner's no-trump. Example: Bidding two no-trump shows about 8-9 points; with 10 or more points, the response should be three no-trump.

Now that the responder has bid three no-trump, that will be the final contract for game. But if the response had been two no-trump, showing 8-9 points, it is easy for the opener in no-trump to gauge the situation. He counts his points. If he has 16, it's not quite enough for game and he leaves the contract at two no-trump. If he has 18 points, he knows he can go to three no-trump with sufficient points. If he has 17 points, he looks over his hand. What is the fit? He knows his partner has strength in at least one major suit; so, if he has the other suits well protected, he can venture a three no-trump bid.

Here's another example in Stayman. You are now the opener, and have originally bid one no-trump. Your partner bid two clubs and you hold the following hand:

♠ 10 6 4 3   ♥ A Q J 8   ♦ A Q   ♣ K 10 4

The bidding so far:

SOUTH	WEST	NORTH	EAST
1 No-Trump	Pass	2 Clubs	Pass

What do you bid? Holding both majors, the normal procedure is to bid spades first. However, your spade suit is not a biddable one. Therefore, your correct bid is two hearts. To bid a major in the Stayman, it should be headed by at least a queen. To stretch it a bit, it could be headed by a jack.

OTHER RESPONSES TO OPENING NO-TRUMP BIDS

To an Opening One No-Trump Bid

Pass. The one no-trump opening bid is not forcing, and if you find yourself with a complete bust, you can pass. An example of this would be the following hand:

♠ 9 7 4 3 2   ♥ 8 6 4 3   ♦ J 9 4   ♣ 10

• You pass and hope that the one no-trump bid has not been doubled for penalty. You don't want to go any further with this junk. One no-trump is high enough with this holding as the opener's partner.

• With unbalanced hands, a response of two diamonds, hearts or spades shows a five-card suit with no interest in going to game.

• Four of a major suit. This response requires 7-9 points and a long major suit. By long, we mean at least six in length. This is a shutout bid and the hand will be played in either four hearts or spades.

To a Two No-Trump Opening Bid

Remember, an opener at two no-trump must have 22-24 high card points. Therefore, if you, as responder, have as little as four points, the total of both hands is at least 26 and sufficient for game. The following is your guide for responses to two no-trump opening bids. With balanced distribution, bid the following:

• Pass with less than four points.

• With 4 to 8 points, raise to three no-trump. Even if you have the maximum of eight points, you know there isn't the possibility of slam. Your partner's 24 points and your 8 points add up to 32 points, still one short of slam requirements, which is 33 points.

• With 9 points, raise to four no-trump. If your partner has the maximum of twenty-four points, your side may be able to go to slam. (24 + 9 = 33 points).

• With 10 points, your side is looking at slam, unless your partner has the absolute minimum of 22 points. What you should do is first bid a suit and then raise to four no-trump. This is stronger than just bidding four no-trump, as you would do with 9 points, and lets your partner know that you have 10 points.

• With 11-12 points, bid six no-trump. Going strictly by the point count, you'll have at least 33 points even if your partner has a minimum holding of 22 high card points. If he should hold as many as 24 points, you still don't have the total of 37 points necessary to bid a grand slam (seven no-trump).

• With 13-14 points, first bid a suit and then bid six no-trump. This is stronger than a direct bid to six no-trump. If your partner has the maximum holding of 24 points, he should bid seven no-trump. If he has only 22 points he will pass your six no-trump bid.

• With 15 points in your hand, you can go directly to

seven no-trump. Even if your partner has a minimum holding of 22 points, 22 + 15 = 37 points. This means that your opponents don't hold an ace.

To a Two No-Trump Opening Bid with Unbalanced Hands

In the previous section, we covered balanced distribution and the possible responses with that kind of hand. However, if you have unbalanced distribution (anything less than a 5-3-3-2 distribution, such as 6-1-2-4) you will have different responses to your partner's opening bid. Here they are:

• If you have a solid six-card major suit, bid it, no matter how few points you have in your hand. If you held a strong heart suit, your response would be three hearts.

• If you have at least 4 points in high cards and a five-card major, bid that suit at the next level.

• With eight points in high cards and a six-card major, jump raise to four in that suit.

To a Three No-Trump Opening Bid

When your partner opens with three no-trump, you know that she is holding between 25-27 points in high cards. Your first thought is a slam, either small or grand. Count the high points in your hand, and see whether your combined total can be as high as 33 for the small slam or 37 for the grand slam.

• With 7 points bid four no-trump.

• With 8-9 points go directly to a bid of six no-trump. Your side will have 36 high card points at the maximum, not enough for a grand slam.

• With 10-11 points, first bid a suit and then rebid six no-trump on the next round. Some experts use the convention of bidding four diamonds in this spot strictly as an artificial bid. This bid is stronger than a direct bid of six no-trump which fully states your hand.

If you go directly to six no-trump, your partner takes it as a shutout bid and will not bid higher. But first bidding four diamonds alerts him to your 10-11 points. If he has 27 high card points, he can go to seven no-trump.
• With twelve points, bid seven no-trump. Even if your partner has the minimum of 25 high card points, there is no ace out against your side (25 + 12 = 37).

OPENING BIDS OF TWO IN A SUIT

Opening the bidding with two in a suit, such as two diamonds or two spades, shows a very powerful hand, good enough to go to game by itself. It is a forcing bid, demanding that the partnership go at least to game contract. When a player has such a strong hand, it is important that he open the bidding at the two-level, since his partner, if she holds less than six points, can pass an opening bid of a suit in the one-level.

Not only must his partner respond to the opening two-bid, but she must keep responding till at least game contract is reached. That's how strong the hand is that is opened in a suit at the two-level.

The following are the requirements for opening in a suit at the two-level:
• Twenty-five points (both high cards and distributional strength) with a good five-card suit. If you hold two good five-card suits, you need only 24 points.
• Twenty-three points with a good six-card suit. A good suit is a strong suit, headed by a couple of high honors.
• Twenty-one points with a good seven-card suit.
• If the hand is to be played in a minor suit, then two more points must be added to the above requirements. For example, if you held a good six-card suit in diamonds, you'd need twenty-five, instead of the twenty-three points necessary if your strong suit was a major,

such as spades. The reason for this rule is that game in a minor suit requires the winning of 11 tricks rather than the ten needed to fulfill a major suit game.

Let's now examine some hands:

♠ 9 ♥ K Q J 10 4 ♦ A K Q 5 ♣ A K J

Your correct bid is two hearts. You have a solid five-card major, twenty-three points in high cards, and an additional two points for the spade singleton; a total of 25 points.

♠ A Q J 9 5 4 ♥ K Q 4 ♦ A K Q ♣ 8

Bid two spades. You have a solid six-card major suit and 21 points in high cards, plus two points for the singleton club. You fill the requirements of 23 points and a good six-card major.

♠ A K Q 10 8 5 3 ♥ A Q 6 ♦ A 7 ♣ 2

Bid two spades. You have 19 points in high cards, plus three additional points in distribution (2 for the club singleton and 1 for the diamond doubleton). Plus you have an outstanding seven-card major suit. Your 22 points exceeds the requirement of 21 points with a good seven-card major.

♠ K Q 5 ♥ A K Q ♦ A K Q 9 4 2 ♣ 5

Bid two diamonds. Since you're in a minor suit, you'll need twenty-five instead of twenty-three points to open at the two-level. You have 23 points in high cards, plus two more in distribution for the club singleton, giving you a total of 25 points, meeting the requirement. The reason that two more points are needed in a minor suit, is that game is eleven tricks, not the ten needed with major suits.

RESPONSES TO OPENING BIDS OF TWO IN A SUIT

The opening bid of two in a suit is forcing to game. No matter what holdings the responder has, he cannot pass. The following are his possible responses:

Two no-trump

This is a very weak bid, showing a poor hand. It is both a negative and artificial bid, telling the opener, "I have nothing or next to nothing." But this doesn't let the responder off the hook. The opener will usually make a rebid showing a second suit, rebid the original suit or raise the no-trump response. The original responder is now forced to make another bid. He cannot just let the bidding die out.

Let's follow a sequence of bids. You are the original bidder of two spades as South and your partner, North, responded with two no-trump. You hold the following hand:

♠ A K Q J 6 5   ♥ A K Q 9 2   ♦ 3   ♣ 4

Your correct bid is now three hearts. You intend to end up in game in either major, and now you wait to see which major your partner prefers by his next bid. If he bids three spades, your final contract will be four spades, bid by you. If he bids hearts, your contract will be in hearts.

However, suppose he now responds with three no-trump, showing no interest in either major suit. You end the bidding with four spades. It's your strongest major and you are at game contract.

Three in the same suit

7-8 points are needed, along with adequate trump support. Unlike the response of two no-trump, which is negative, this is a positive response, inviting your partner to explore slam possibilities.

A bid of three in another suit

This is a natural bid showing strength in that suit. If a major is named and is of five or more cards in length, responder will bid it twice, showing its strength. If the original opener has a fit in that major, he will bid till slam, with that suit as trump. 7-8 points are needed by responder to bid a new suit in this fashion. This is a positive response.

Three no-trump

Responder shows at least 9 points and no suit to bid. In other words, responder has no biddable five-card suit and he doesn't hold at least four cards in opener's suit. The following is a hand that should be responded to in three no-trump after opener's bid of two hearts.

♠ Q 7 5 4   ♥ 8 6   ♦ K 9 8 7   ♣ A 9 5

There are nine points in high cards, no biddable five-card suit and his heart holding is weak. This doesn't end the bidding, for now opener knows that with his 25 point holding and partner's nine points, he has enough to try for slam.

5. OPENER'S REBIDS

An opener's rebid can be defined as the second bid of the opener. In this section, we're dealing with suit bids that began at the one level, such as one diamond or one spade. The rebid is an important part of the bidding process, and often determines just where the contract is going, whether to a partial score, game or slam.

After the partner responded, the opener has a choice of rebids. We'll examine the responses one at a time, and determine just what rebid the opener should make.

AFTER A ONE OVER ONE RESPONSE

To refresh our recollection, a one over one response indicates that the responder has six to seventeen points and four or more cards in the bid suit.

• Rebid one no-trump with 13-15 points and a balanced hand.

• Rebid the opening suit with a strong five-card suit and 12-16 points.

• Rebid the responder's suit if you hold four cards in his suit and 12-16 points. A good example of this bid would be the following hand. You've opened the bidding with one heart and your partner has responded with one spade. You hold these cards:

♠ Q J 9 5   ♥ A Q J 6 4   ♦ A 7   ♣ J 4

Your best bet here is to support the responder's spades by bidding two spades.

• Jump bid to two no-trump, or jump in your own or partner's suit with 17-19 points. For example, if you opened with one diamond and your partner responded with one heart, and you hold 18 points and a four-card heart suit, jump to three hearts.

• Jump to game in responder's major suit if you hold a relatively balanced hand with 19-20 points, and four cards in responder's suit. The following diagram would show the bidding to game. You are South and the opener; your partner has responded with a one spade bid.

SOUTH	WEST	NORTH	EAST
1 Diamond	Pass	1 Spade	Pass
4 Spades			

• Jump shift rebid. For example, if you opened with one diamond, and your partner responded with one spade, a bid of three clubs is a jump shift rebid to a new suit. This rebid shows 19-20 points, an unbalanced hand, and is forcing to game. Here's a typical holding:

♠ A J 8 3   ♥ 7   ♦ A Q J 5 4   ♣ A Q 5

You can show your spade fit on the next rebid.

AFTER A ONE NO-TRUMP RESPONSE

By responding one no-trump, your partner has shown 6-10 honor points (high card points) and no biddable suit at the one level. Here's how the opener should rebid his hand:

- With 12-15 points and balanced distribution, he should pass.
- With 12-15 points and unbalanced distribution, he can rebid his suit or a new good suit. The same holds true if he holds 16-18 points.
- With 18-19 points, the opener should raise to two no-trump or jump to three of a suit, either his originally bid suit or a good new one.
- With 20 points or more, the opener should raise to three no-trump or bid at the three-level in a new suit.

Let's examine some representative hands. You are the opener and have opened with one spade, sitting as South. Your partner has responded with one no-trump. You hold the following hand:

♠ K Q J 8 5 4   ♥ K J 7   ♦ 5   ♣ A Q 7

Bid three spades. You have 16 points in high cards plus two points for the singleton diamond. By jumping the bid to three spades, you are giving your partner the option of going to game. If he holds but 6 or 7 points, he should pass, but with 8-10 points, he should bid four spades and go to game.

♠ A K 10 4 3   ♥ A Q 6   ♦ K 5   ♣ A 8 4

Bid three no-trump. Your hand contains twenty points in high cards, and you know your partner has at least six points, so a game bid is in order.

AFTER A TWO OVER ONE RESPONSE

Your partner has shown a good suit, with five or more cards, and at least 10 honor points, with a possible 18 points, counting distributional strength.

  • With 12-16 points, make a minimum rebid at the two level, or rebid partner's suit at the three level. The weakest of the rebids is two of your own suit. You make this bid when you hold only 12-14 points, and want to discourage your partner from going too far.

  • With 17-19 points, make a jump bid at the three level or bid a new suit at the three level. This is a powerful rebid and is encouraging.

  • With 20 or more points, bid game or make a bid forcing to game, such as a jump bid in a new suit.

REBID AFTER A SINGLE RAISE IN OPENER'S MAJOR SUIT

Your partner's response shows he has 7-10 points and three or four trumps.

  • 12-15 points in your hand. Pass.

  • 16-18 points. Depending upon your distribution, bid three of your suit, or two no-trump. If you're thinking of game, you can bid a new suit, which is forcing, and to which your partner must respond with other than a pass.

  • 19 or more points; jump to game or jump bid a new suit.

REBID AFTER A DOUBLE RAISE IN A MAJOR SUIT

Your partner has 13-16 points and a four card trump holding, headed by at least a queen.

  • 12-16 points. You are aiming for game here, for a slam is very unlikely. Bid three no-trump with balanced distribution or four in your major suit. The bidding will stop at game.

  • 17 or more points. You're thinking of a possible slam. See Section on Slam Bidding.

REBID AFTER A TRIPLE RAISE
IN A MAJOR SUIT

Your partner will have only 10 points at best. Pass unless you can see slam possibilities with more than twenty points in your hand, with at least three aces. Again, see Section on Slam Bidding.

RESPONDER'S REBIDS

Having heard two bids from the opener, the opening bid and the rebid, you, as responder, should have some idea of your partner's strength. You must now assess your hand and see whether you will attempt to get a part score, a game score, or possibly go for a slam.

Unless you've been forced to keep the bidding alive, or to go for game, the following is a good guide to follow:

• 6-10 points. Make one response and don't bid again unless your partner forces you to.

• 11-13 points. You can make two bids for you have a decent hand that could very well go to game.

• 13-17 points. Your hand is equal to your partner's in that you could have made an opening bid yourself. With this type of strength, you must make certain that your side gets to game.

• 18 or more points. You must think about a slam with this kind of strength. The ideal way to show this strength to your partner is to jump bid a new suit. If you have 20 points you should be assured of a slam bid, for adding your partner's 13 points to yours, gives you 33, enough for a small slam.

6. PRE-EMPTIVE OR SHUT-OUT BID

An opening bid of three, four or five in a suit is a **pre-emptive** or **shut-out bid**. These bids are made with hands that are relatively weak in high strength, and their primary purpose is to destroy the lines of communication of the opponents. What the pre-emptive bidder fears is that the opponents have powerful hands, and if left unimpeded, their bidding might even take them to slam levels. By throwing in the pre-emptive bid, he hopes to force the opponents to possibly overbid their hands at high levels, or force them to bid inaccurately, at the same high levels.

There is a danger in making a pre-emptive bid. The shut-out bidder may be doubled by the opponents, and be set by several tricks, with many penalty points going to the other side. That is the basic negative of a pre-emptive bid. It must be weighed in those terms. How many points will the bidder be penalized, as against how many points has he saved his side by preventing the other partnership from bidding and making a slam.

The two constants of the hand that the pre-emptive bidder has are: it will be lacking in high cards, and it will contain a long suit. Most experts agree that a pre-emptive bid should never be made with a hand containing more than 9 points in high cards when not vulnerable, and no more than 10 points in high cards when vulnerable. This is known as the "safety" factor. A player making a shut-out bid must be prepared to be doubled and lose points. However, he should limit his losses to 500 points at the most. This means overbidding by three tricks when not vulnerable, and two tricks when vulnerable. In either event, the loss is 500 points.

When making a pre-emptive bid, you are assuming that you will be doubled, that you will go down a number of tricks, and that your partner has absolutely nothing to help your hand. Therefore, you'll win only those tricks you see in your hand. Here's a good method of figuring out the potential tricks needed.

• With an opening bid of three in a suit, we need to win in our hand six tricks when not vulnerable, and seven tricks when vulnerable. Or put another way, we can afford to go down three tricks when not vulnerable, and only two tricks when vulnerable.

• With an opening bid of four in a suit, we need to win seven tricks from our own hand when not vulnerable and eight tricks when vulnerable.

• With an opening bid of five in a suit, we must win eight tricks from our own hand when not vulnerable, and nine if vulnerable.

Here are some examples of pre-emptive bidding hands: (x = indifferent or low card, such as a 2-8)

♠ K Q J x x x x x   ♥ x   ♦ x x   ♣ x x

If not vulnerable, the correct pre-emptive bid is four spades. If vulnerable, only three spades. At four spades, not vulnerable, there is an overbid of three tricks. At three spades, vulnerable, there is an overbid of two tricks. In either event, if doubled, the loss is 500 points.

♠ x   ♥ Q J 10 9   ♦ x   ♣ Q J 10 9 x x x

Your hand can win five club tricks and two heart tricks. Your bid would be four clubs if not vulnerable, or three clubs if vulnerable.

When you make a pre-emptive bid, you must realize you are sacrificing yourself, and being penalized, but more often than not, you'll be disrupting the opponents and saving points in the long run by preventing them from bidding and making slam contracts.

7. SLAM BIDDING

Correct slam bidding is an essential tool for a bridge player, for many bonus points are at stake everytime there's the possibility of a slam bid and made. In rubber bridge, the bonuses run from 500 to 1,500 points, and therefore can make the difference between a winning or losing session. In duplicate bridge, where each hand is important, because your partnership is playing against a large number of other partnerships, it is of the same importance, because the side that is able to bid and make a slam, when it is the correct contract, will get the most points for this accomplishment.

There are two essential elements involved in slam bidding; strength and controls. These two elements must be present, because a small slam requires the winning of twelve tricks and a grand slam, all the tricks. **Strength** means a high-point count; **control** refers to absolute domination of a suit or suits by either an ace or a void.

STRENGTH

There are forty points in high cards in the deck, and it is usually essential that the partners in a slam contract have at least 33 of them. When a no-trump contract is bid, it is mandatory that there be those 33 high cards between the two partners, because power cards are important in no-trump games. There are no trumps; therefore potential losing cards cannot be trumped if a void develops.

In suit contracts, the same 33 points in high cards need not always be present for a small slam. For example, if there is a void or a singleton, that may be sufficient to stop the defenders from cashing two tricks and setting the contract. Sometimes the best slam contracts in suits develop from unbalanced hands; where one of the partners has a very long suit, a solid second suit, and a void and singleton in the other suits. Or he may have two singletons, as in the next hand.

♠ A K Q J 8 6 4 2 ♥ 6 ♦ 5 ♣ A K Q

Obviously, this is a very powerful hand, almost able to go to slam by itself, if the declarer had the first lead. But by the rules of bridge, the defenders lead first and two aces are missing. If the defenders hold the aces and correctly lead them, the contract will be set at once, going down one trick. But if the partner of the holder of the above hand has one ace, either in hearts or diamonds, a small slam can certainly be bid and probably made. The only hindrance would be a disastrous split in trumps of 5-0 in the hands of the defenders. This would occur 4% of the time.

However, if declarer's partner has one trump and one ace, the small slam contract is assured. If the partner has both aces and one trump, a grand slam is assured. Even if the partner has no trumps, declarer must go for the slam if partner has one or two aces; he is 96% certain of getting a favorable split in trumps.

KEY CARDS

We might therefore say, that in this instance, the **key cards** to the slam are the two missing aces. If the partner has only four points in his entire hand, but it consists of one of the aces, then at least a small slam can be bid. If partner has both aces, and a total of 8 high card points, a grand slam can be bid. Without either ace in partner's hand, there is no slam, period. Suppose the declarer's partner held the following hand:

♠ 3　♥ K Q J 5 4　♦ K Q J　♣ J 9 7 5

He has a lovely hand with 13 high cards and 15 points altogether, but there's no possibility of slam. The aces are missing.

Other key cards that are taken into consideration in slam bidding are the kings, the singletons and the voids. As we saw with the aces in the previous hand, they may become more important than mere points. Thus, with key cards falling into place, fewer than 33 points may be needed to bid a small slam, or less than 37 for a grand slam. If one ace is out against you, but you're void in that suit, you negate the power of the opponent's strength.

Long, powerful trump suits are excellent for slam bidding because once the opponents' trumps are used up the smaller trump cards are automatic winners. Likewise a long and strong second suit is quite valuable, because after all the opponents' trumps are gone, the declarer can then cash in that side suit, winning tricks.

When you hold a long powerful trump suit and a long side suit, your hand will be unbalanced, and you'll probably have a void or singleton, or combination of the two. As we noted, voids and singletons are keys to slam bidding.

CONTROLS

Since the opponents, the defenders, play the first card, leading toward dummy, if they hold one ace in a grand slam contract or two aces in a small slam contract, they may be able to win their tricks immediately and defeat the contract. Therefore it's essential to have **controls**, cards such as aces which rule a particular suit, or a void, which allows the declarer to trump the led ace of the opponents. These are first-round controls and are always necessary in slams. Second-round controls are also valuable in small-slam bids. A second-round control would be the king of a suit or a singleton, keys that we have mentioned before.

Therefore, it is extremely important in bidding a slam to examine what controls you do have and what you are missing. In those instances where you hold all the controls, the slam bid is a breeze. But this is an extremely rare situation. Basically you'll be dependent upon the controls that your partner has; his aces and kings. There is a way to get this information, and that is the Blackwood Convention.

BLACKWOOD CONVENTION

This convention, which was invented by Easley Blackwood in 1933, has been accepted by bridge players the world over as a method to discover how many aces and kings the partner holds. It starts with an artificial bid of four no-trump, asking for aces, and if the bidder needs to know the number of kings his partner holds, then he continues with a five no-trump bid.

By the time the bidding reaches this level, the partnership has agreed on a trump suit, or no-trump, and either partner can ask for aces using the Blackwood. As a general rule, the partner with the strongest hand will bid four no-trump, since he will be the only one with a clear picture of just how many aces the partnership holds, once the partner responds. The bidder at Blackwood should feel that he can make eleven tricks, for he is bidding at a rather high level, and the response will be at the five-level.

Once four no-trump has been bid, the bidder's partner will answer as follows, depending upon how many aces he holds in his hand. When players agree on using Blackwood as a bidding convention, the partner cannot pass the four no-trump bid; he is forced to respond according to the convention. Here are the responses to the four no-trump bid:

No aces or four aces	five clubs
One ace	five diamonds
Two aces	five hearts
Three aces	five spades

It will be rare for the responder to have all four aces, for by the time the partners have reached this level of bidding, the Blackwood bidder should have at least one ace and probably more. But if showing all four aces entailed a bid of five no-trump, it would preclude that bid asking for kings.

After receiving his information about the aces held by his partner, now kings can be asked for. This bid is five no-trump, again an artificial bid and again forcing. Here's what the various responses mean to the bid of five no-trump.

No kings	six clubs
One king	six diamonds
Two kings	six hearts
Three kings	six spades
Four kings	six no-trump

Let's now go back to the hand we illustrated at the beginning of this section.

♠ A K Q J 8 6 4 2   ♥ 6   ♦ 5   ♣ A K Q

The holder of this hand is missing two aces, and his only interest is knowing if his partner holds one or both of them, so he can bid a small slam or go to a grand slam. Using the Blackwood Convention, he now bids four no-trump.

Should his partner respond with a bid of five diamonds, he knows that he has one ace, and therefore, the final bid will be for a small slam, at six spades. There's no point in asking for kings with his hand; they'll play no role in improving his prospects for a grand slam. The only consideration here were the aces. Had his partner responded with five hearts, then he would have an automatic bid of seven spades, hoping that his partner wasn't void in trump, and if so, that the split wasn't 5-0 against him. That would be the only way he could lose the contract.

When your partner bids four no-trump, he is asking for aces. You should respond according to the formula stated above, naming your exact ace holding. If you are void in a suit, you cannot bid it as if it were an ace. This will lead to great difficulties and you'll have a partner furious at you. If you hold one ace and are void in a suit, the response is still five diamonds, showing one ace.

A final note: Whoever bids four no-trump is the captain of the ship; he will know, from his partner's response, just how many aces are in both hands, and if he bids five no-trump, he will have the same information about kings. He must make the final bid; the responder cannot do so. If the Blackwood bidder stops at six, that's where the contract will be. His partner, no matter what his reasoning, cannot bid higher. He must obey the captain of the partnership and his judgment in this situation.

CUE BIDS

A cue bid can be used to go to slam, in situations where the Blackwood Convention isn't used. When a player holds a void in a suit that won't be trump, a number of experts avoid the Blackwood for fear of bidding too high. Let's examine a typical situation that illustrates this principle. We'll follow the bidding of two partners, North and South.

NORTH	SOUTH
♠ -	♠ Q J 8 6 5
♥ A K J 9 8 4	♥ 5 3
♦ A 10 9	♦ K Q J 8 4 2
♣ A Q 10 6	♣ -

We first note that North is void in spades and South in clubs. During the bidding each partner will cue the other as to the control he has in the void suit. We'll mark these cues with bold lettering. The bidding was as follows:

NORTH	SOUTH
Two hearts	Two no-trump
Three hearts	Four diamonds
Four spades	**Five clubs**
Six diamonds	Seven diamonds

The use of cue bids (four spades, five clubs) was necessary here in order for the partners to reach a grand slam.

In Blackwood, if North had bid four no-trump, South's response would have been five clubs, showing no aces. He had no way to show his void, and the final bid would have been six diamonds. Here, by the use of cue bids, the partners reached a grand slam that was a certainty to make.

The cue bid can also prevent a slam by the information it conveys. In the next example, North cued his ace of clubs, asking partner if he wished to go to slam. We'll show the cue bid in bold letters.

NORTH	SOUTH
♠ 10 3	♠ K Q 9 5
♥ A Q J 9 4	♥ 10 6 5 3
♦ Q J 5	♦ K 3
♣ A J 7	♣ K Q 6

The bidding went:

NORTH	SOUTH
One heart	Three hearts
Four clubs	Four hearts

North made his cue bid at the first opportunity, showing his stopper in clubs, and thus asked partner if there was a chance to go to slam. South, without an ace in his hand, stops at game.

8. MODERN BRIDGE CONVENTIONS

As the years go by, and the game of bridge has matured, it has become more complicated. There have been a plethora of bidding conventions invented and popularized by various players, partnerships and teams. Some are very complex; others are so esoteric that a situation to use a particular convention might come up twice in one year for a team that plays constantly.

What we are endeavoring to do in this book is show you the basic standard conventions that have stood the test of time and are universally played. These include, but are not limited to Stayman, Blackwood, Five-Card Majors and so forth.

As you become more experienced at bridge, you might want to examine and study other bidding conventions. First you need a steady partner, for you would want to study these conventions together. It's of no use to memorize a complex convention, only to find that your partner has no idea what it's all about. As you play more often; especially if you play in duplicate tournaments, you'll be asked to put down the conventions you use. It's perfectly all right to put down Stayman, Blackwood and Five Card-Majors. They have stood the test of time, and are valuable tools that will make you a better player.

While you may have limited your bidding conventions, you will come across partners who will put down or state to you that they play a number of complicated conventions, some of which you might not even have heard about. It is their obligation to explain them to you if you don't know just how they work.

When you play with one partner, you may find that your style of game lends itself to a particular convention or two. Examine them and see if they work for both of you. There are books just devoted to bidding conventions; after some experience, you might want to dip into them. In the meantime study the principles shown in this book; they'll make you a stronger player.

9. DEFENSIVE BIDDING

Up to this point, we've examined opening bids and responses, showing just what hands to open at various levels and what responses should be made to those opening bids. We've also examined rebids, the use of some bidding conventions and opening bids of an unique nature, such as the pre-emptive bid. We've also discussed how to get to slam, the requirements for slam bidding, and conventions, such as Blackwood and Cue Bidding, that will help you in your endeavor to bid slam contracts. Now we're going to focus on defensive bidding.

By defensive bidding, we mean those situations where the opponents have opened the bidding, and you put in a bid or bids to challenge for the contract. It may come at the first level of bidding or later, and it isn't limited to just suit or no-trump bids; doubles are a valid bid as well, both as penalty bids and as takeouts, which disrupt the opponents' orderly bidding as you show your card strength.

When the other side opens the bidding, it isn't often that you may be able to interject bids. They'll have the card strength and the initiative in bidding; many times all you and your partner will do is pass, pass and once more pass, as the other side merrily moves on their way to a game or slam contract. There's nothing you can do about those situations. Often novices, holding rather weak hands, just throw in a bid, thinking to disrupt the bidding process of the other side, only to be doubled and punished with over a thousand penalty points.

GOALS OF DEFENSIVE BIDDING

Bidding defensively, you must be selective. You must find your spots, and then act. When you are holding some strength in cards, you should bid for the following reasons:

• You think you have a competitive hand and are going for a part score for your side.

• Your competitive bids drive the other side into a higher contract than they can make.

• Sacrificing a hand that will go down only a couple of tricks will be better than letting your opponents make game or higher.

• Bidding a suit so as to signal your partner to lead that suit.

Against these factors, you must weigh the word "double" and the dire consequences that word and subsequent action entail. You don't want to take a bloodbath in penalty points; again, we urge that you be selective. We'll discuss a number of defensive bidding strategies in this section, and show you how to handle them correctly, for optimum results.

OVERCALLS

An **overcall** is a defensive tactic in which the player to the left of the opener, makes a bid of a suit or no-trump. For example, the following is an overcall of one spade by West.

SOUTH	WEST	NORTH	EAST
1 Heart	1 Spade		

If West had a strong minor suit, he could have over-called at two clubs or two diamonds. When the bidder to the opener's left bids this way, he is overcalling at the two-level, and the requirements for an overcall are a little more stringent, because another trick has to be won at the higher level. Here are a number of requirements necessary for an overcall:

a. 13-16 points. Above this level in points, as we shall see in the appropriate section, a double is preferred. Some experts feel that fewer points are necessary if one holds a suit of six cards. Since the overcall is a defensive bid against an opener, the overcaller should be prepared to play the hand if doubled. Therefore, if he is overcalling at the two-level, six cards should be in his bid suit.

Another factor to consider is vulnerability. If the op-posing side is vulnerable, and you are not, then you can stretch the opening strength required down to ten points, with a six-card suit. Thus, overcalls are sometimes made at these weak point levels, when the opponents have a partial score. They may be reluctant to double the overcall, want-ing instead to bid their own suits and make game.

b. An overcall should be made with at least a five-card holding, and even better, a six-card trump hand. As stated above, when overcalling at the two-level, a six-card suit is almost mandatory. That is because if the bid is doubled, the overcaller has to make that extra trick at the two-level.

c. The honor strength in the bid suit should be at least a five-card suit headed by A-K, K-Q, K-J or Q-J. Therefore avoid an overcall if your bid suit contains cards such as Q 9 5 4 3. Even a Q-J five-card suit might give you trouble, but if it were Q J 10 9 5 3, the 10 and 9 strengthen it consider-ably.

d. If your side is vulnerable, you must be more careful with overcalls. A double and a consequential set of the bid hand may carry with it too many penalty points to make the overcall worthwhile. Always feel freer to make an overcall when the opponents are vulnerable and you are not.

Overcalls not only can obstruct the opponents' bidding but also they serve as a lead signal to partner. The defenders always lead first, and an opening lead is rather crucial in many cases, determining whether the other side's contract can be set. Once you overcall, you're directing partner to lead your bid suit; otherwise he'll lead his own best suit. That's why we showed how important the honors holding is when bidding an overcall. Let's look at such an example.

You are West and non-vulnerable. South has opened with one diamond. You hold the following cards:

♠ Q 9 5 4 3
♥ Q J 5
♦ 7 6
♣ K Q 3

You should pass. Your five-card suit is led only by a queen, much too weak a suit for an overcall. If you do bid two spades, your partner will lead a spade to you, instead of leading his best suit, which might be hearts or clubs, where your honors would better help him establish his own strong suit.

Another example: Again, South has opened with one diamond and you hold the following cards as West. Your side isn't vulnerable.

♠ K Q J 8 7 3
♥ 10 9 4
♦ 7 5
♣ K 10

By overcalling here, you're stretching the minimum requirement a bit, only holding eleven points but you have a good solid six-card spade suit, and your bid of one spade directs your partner to lead that suit.

To summarize, an overcall is a fine defensive tool, which serves one or more of the following purposes:
- It may stop the opponents from arriving at a game contract.
- It can be used to outbid attempted part scores or possibly game contracts by the opposing side.
- It has nuisance value, depriving the opponents of the chance to exchange bidding information at a low level.
- It directs the correct lead by your partner into your best suit.

DOUBLES

When we first described all the bids possible in bridge, we mentioned doubles, both penalty and takeout doubles. The **penalty double** is bid to punish the opponents for bidding too high. It is made when you or your partner feel you can set the contract and garner penalty points. The **takeout double** has different implications; it is bid to show a hand containing opening strength held by the doubler with the possibility of arriving at your own contract. Let's first focus on this type of double.

TAKEOUT DOUBLES

A **takeout double** is made in low-levels of bidding, forcing your partner to bid his best suit. This bid avoids naming a suit before your partner has responded. When made at the one or two level after the opening bid or the response to the opening bid, providing all the parameters as stated below are met, it cannot be construed as a penalty double.

The following are the parameters necessary to show a takeout double.

• It must be made at bidder's first opportunity to double an opponent's bid suit. The following is a good example of this:

SOUTH	WEST	NORTH	EAST
1 Heart	Double		

• It should be made at the one or two-level of bidding, as West's double in the above example.

• The doubler's partner has not bid yet.

Let's look at another example of a double:

SOUTH	WEST	NORTH	EAST
1 Heart	Pass	2 Clubs	Pass
2 Hearts	Double		

In this example, we see that two of the criteria have been met; it was bid at the second level and doubler's partner has not yet bid. But it is not a takeout double. The double wasn't bid at bidder's (West) first opportunity. It must therefore be construed as a penalty double.

Here are the card requirements necessary to make a takeout double:
  • At least 13 points (opening strength).
  • Support for whatever suit his partner may bid, if doubler has no good biddable suit of his own, or a strong suit of his own to play the contract in.

Let's look at a couple of examples. You are sitting West and South has opened the bidding with one spade. Your cards are:

♠ 8 ♥ K Q 8 5 ♦ K J 9 4 ♣ A J 9 3

You have fourteen points in high cards plus the spade singleton. You really don't know which suit is your partner's best. You'd prefer to play the hand in a major suit (hearts), but you only have four cards in that suit; so you double the one spade bid, forcing your partner to name his best suit. Whatever he names, whether it be clubs, diamonds or hearts, the unbid suits, you'll have sufficient trumps to support him. In this case, if you reach a part or game contract, your partner will play out the hand, since he bid the best suit first, and you'll be dummy.

Let's now look at another hand. You're West and South has just opened with one spade. You hold the following cards:

♠ 7 2 ♥ A K J 10 5 4 ♦ A 8 6 ♣ K 3

You may be tempted to overcall with two hearts, but if you go back to our discussion of overcalls, we set a parameter of 13-16 points to overcall. Above that, we stated, a double would be preferable. Here we have 17 points (15 in high cards, plus the two doubletons). The correct bid is a double. No matter what partner answers, you can always play out the hand in your powerful hearts suit.

A final note: When you bid a takeout double, your partner is forced to bid for *one round only*. He may have absolute garbage in his hand, but he must bid. After his forcing bid, he is not required to make any other rebids.

RESPONSES TO TAKEOUT DOUBLES

Whenever your partner bids a takeout double, you are required (forced) to respond for at least one round. You cannot pass. Thereafter, as mentioned before, you are no longer under any obligation to rebid. However, there is one exception to this rule, and that is a **penalty pass**, where you are allowing the takeout double to stand as a penalty double.

Let's examine the options open to the takeout doubler's partner.

A. The penalty pass. Pass only if you have a long suit in opener's bid suit, and at least four winning tricks in your hand. Otherwise, you cannot pass. Let's examine a situation that would be right for a penalty pass. The bidding has gone as follows:

South has opened with one heart, West, your partner, has doubled, North has passed, and you, as East, hold the following hand:

♠ 9 5 ♥ K Q J 9 5 ♦ 9 8 5 4 ♣ A 3

With the above hand you can pass. You should be able

to make three tricks in hearts and another in clubs. Also, your partner has at least an opening hand and should contribute at least three more tricks, enough to set the contract of one heart.

B. 0-8 points. Bid at the lowest level you can. If the opening bid had been one diamond, and partner doubled, bid either one heart, one spade or two clubs. If you hold the following hand, a minimum bid would be in order.

♠ 8 5 4   ♥ J 6 4 3   ♦ 6 5   ♣ 8 6 4 2

Basically, your hand is a complete bust, but you cannot pass your partner's double. You must bid something. You bid your best suit and respond with one heart. You're not promising your partner anything; and this bid should tell your partner not to go any further in the bidding, especially if he opened with a minimum holding.

C. With 9-11 points, you can make a jump response. This bid is not forcing on partner, that is; he need not rebid. If faced with the choice of two good suits, choose a major. The next hand illustrates this situation. The bidding has gone as follows, with you sitting as East:

SOUTH	WEST	NORTH	EAST
1 Heart	Double	Pass	?

You hold the following hand:
♠ K J 5 4   ♥ 9 8 7   ♦ 5 4   ♣ K Q 10 9

Bid two spades. You have a slightly stronger club suit than your holding in spades, but bid the major, even though it's only four cards. Since the bidding was at the one level, your bid is a jump response. It is not forcing on partner but instead invites him to try for game in spades if he has a good spade suit and more than the minimum points for opening.

D. With 12 or more points, make a **cue bid**, that is, bid the opener's suit, showing your partner that your side has enough for game. With less than 14 points, simply rebid at the minimum level. With 14 points or more, jump rebid at the next opportunity.

PENALTY DOUBLES

Unlike the takeout double, the penalty double is used to penalize the opposing side for bidding incorrectly. When your partner bids a double, you should be able to distinguish between the double as takeout or penalty. Remember that in order to be a takeout double it must be made at doubler's first opportunity, and made before you put in a bid. Let's suppose that you are West and the bidding has gone:

SOUTH	WEST	NORTH	EAST
1 Diamond	Pass	1 Heart	Pass
2 Hearts	Pass	Pass	Double

Even though you haven't yet bid, your partner didn't double at the first opportunity, which was after North's bid of one heart. Therefore you must construe the double as a penalty double.

A double for penalty is used by good players after an overcall, often with devastating effect. Even though the double is at an early level in the bidding, it still must be considered as a penalty double, because the doubler's partner has already bid, therefore taking the double out of takeout and placing it in the penalty category. The following bidding sequence shows this.

SOUTH	WEST	NORTH	EAST
1 Diamond	1 Spade	Double	

Since North's partner has already bid, the double is a penalty double. Many novices are afraid to double contracts at the one-level, but doubles of overcalls often yield a great many penalty points. In this situation, it may be that North has a good hand, with a strong spade suit of his own, and East has a complete busted hand, with just one or two honor points. West may be set several tricks, and if vulnerable, may be penalized hundreds of points.

When a no-trump contract is doubled, even though the double is made at the first opportunity and before a partner has put in a contractual bid (suit or no-trump) it is considered a penalty double, not a takeout. Thus, remember this - all doubles of no-trump contracts are for penalty, even at the one-level.

QUICK TRICKS

When thinking of a penalty double, many experts place more reliance on quick tricks than they do on the point count. A **quick trick** is a trick that can be won on a particular round of play. For example, an ace is a quick trick, since it is the highest ranking card of a suit. An ace and king combined make for two quick tricks, since, if opponents aren't void in the suit, their lower ranking cards must fall to these honors. The following is a list of quick tricks:

A K	2 quick tricks
A Q	1 1/2 quick tricks
A	1 quick trick
K Q	1 quick trick
K x	1/2 quick trick

Sometimes these quick values can be enhanced, depending upon the opponent's bidding. For example, if you hold A Q of a suit bid by the player to your right, who must lead to you, the A Q can be promoted to two quick tricks. The bidder to your right in all probability holds the king of the suit, and must play or lead that suit into your A Q. Therefore, you'll be able to make both the ace and queen as winning tricks. When that suit is led by any other player, the holder of the king, if he plays it, will lose it to your ace, and then your queen is the highest ranking card of the suit. If he doesn't play it, then you play your queen and win the trick, since the player to your right can't beat the queen. This is known as a **finesse**, making a trick because of the favorable position of your cards in relation to the opponents' cards.

Should the bidder of the suit in which you hold, K x, be to your right, you can promote the king from 1/2 a quick trick to a full trick for the same reason. Should your partner or any other player play that suit, if the player to your right plays his ace, then your king is now the highest ranking card of the suit. If he **ducks,** not playing the ace, then you can play the king and win the trick.

On the other hand, if you hold A Q of a suit, and the bidder of that suit is to your left, you can reduce the quick trick value from 1 1/2 to 1, since a lead through you, that is a lead by the player to your right will force you to play the ace to win the trick. If you play the queen, it will fall to the bidder's king. Since he bid the suit, we have to assume he holds the king of that suit.

So, using the Quick Trick table, figure out the number of tricks you can make, adding or subtracting according to the placement of other honors according to opponents' bidding. Now, you must figure out the number of tricks you can depend on from your partner. Here is a quick guide. Your partner has opened the bidding as follows:

QUICK TRICK TABLE

One in a suit	He should win three tricks.
One no-trump	He should win four tricks.
Takeout double	He should win three tricks.
Overcall one-level	He should win one trick.
Overcall two-level	He should win two tricks.

If you've opened the bidding, here is a good guide, according to partner's positive responses (bids of suit or no-trump).

One positive response	He should win one trick.
Two positive responses	He should win two tricks.
Three positive responses	He should win three tricks.

Let's now look at a representative situation. The bidding has gone as follows, with you sitting North.

SOUTH	WEST	NORTH	EAST
1 Spade	2 Hearts	?	

You hold the following cards:

♠ 8 6   ♥ Q J 10 8 6   ♦ A Q 6 2   ♣ K 4

Now, according to our guide above, we add up our quick tricks. We get 1 1/2 tricks for our A Q of diamonds, and 1/2 trick for our K of clubs. That's a total of three tricks. Even though our guiding table didn't allow for the Q J of a suit, we hold Q J 10 8 6 of hearts, which will ensure us of three tricks in hearts. Once the ace and king of hearts is played, and we deplete the 8 and 6, our Q J 10 will be winning tricks. We must be resilient in figuring our tricks. In this situation, with our strong heart suit, we are assured of three tricks in trumps. This now gives us five quick tricks. Since our partner has opened the bidding at the one-level in a suit, we count on her for another three tricks. This gives us eight tricks.

Our opponent's bid of two clubs obligates him to make eight tricks, but by our count, he can only make five. We have a good penalty double here, also called a **business double**.

OTHER REQUIREMENTS

Experts have also figured another way to decide whether or not to double for penalty, when the bidding by the opponents is at a low level of two in a suit. You should have the following:

- 10 points, or more.
- The winning of at least one trump trick.
- Shortness in opener's suit.
- At least 1 1/2 tricks in the unbid suits.

Let's now return to our representative holding to see if it qualifies under these criteria.

♠ 8 6　♥ Q J 10 8 6　♦ A Q 6 2　♣ K 4

The hand holds 12 honor points, at least three winning trump tricks, and 1 1/2 and possibly more tricks in the unbid suits. It certainly fits the criteria for a double.

Although correct doubles yield large profits in penalty points, there is a danger in bidding penalty doubles when you feel that you can set the contract by only one trick, after adding up your points and quick tricks. It just isn't worth it to set a contract one trick. Also, be aware that if you double a major suit contract at the two-level, and the contract is made, you've doubled your opponents into game, worth at least 500 points.

Therefore, it is easier to double a minor suit contract of two, because it will yield only a part score if made. Count your quick tricks carefully, especially your trump tricks. If you can't make a single trump trick, don't double the contract. If you can make one, and possibly two trump tricks, you are on much surer ground for the penalty double.

DOUBLING THREE NO-TRUMP CONTRACTS

When a player not on lead, that is, the one who will not play the first card towards dummy's hand, doubles a three no-trump contract, he is informing his partner of the correct opening lead.

   • If the doubler has bid a suit, his partner must lead that suit, even if he only holds a singleton, and has a strong suit of his own.
   • If the player to lead the first card has bid a suit, then the double informs him to lead that suit. This happens when the doubler hasn't bid a suit.

• If neither the leader nor the doubler have bid, the lead should be in dummy's first bid suit, unless the leader has a good suit of his own to lead.

Let's look at a couple of examples:

WEST	NORTH	EAST	SOUTH
1 Club	1 Heart	1 No Trump	Pass
3 No Trump	Double	Pass	Pass
Pass			

North wants his partner to lead a heart. Her partner must open with doubler's bid suit.

One more example:

WEST	NORTH	EAST	SOUTH
1 Club	1 Diamond	1 Heart	Pass
1 No Trump	Pass	3 No Trump	Double
Pass	Pass	Pass	

North has the first lead, and should play a diamond.

Since South hasn't bid a suit, his double requests North to lead his bid suit, which is diamonds.

DOUBLES OF SLAM CONTRACTS

When the opponents have reached a slam contract, it is probable that they can make at least eleven tricks, and together they should have strong hands and a good fit. It really doesn't pay to double a slam contract just for some measly points above the line if you can possibly, without any degree of certainty, set them by one trick.

Therefore, experts have used the double of a slam contract as a signal to the leader (the one to lead the first card) to make an unusual lead to dummy. By unusual lead, we mean the following: Suppose you and your partner have each bid a suit. Depending upon what you're holding, if on the lead, you'd ordinarily play a card from your bid suit or your partner's bid suit. But his double is telling you, "Partner, wait a second, lead something else, something unusual."

In the typical doubling of a slam, it calls for the leader to play a card of the first suit bid by dummy, unless that suit was trumps. Therefore, the leader must lead the suit which was the first sidesuit (not a trump) bid by dummy. For example, suppose North will be the dummy. The contract is in six spades.

South opened with one spade and North's response was three spades. Then after South bid four clubs, North responded with four diamonds. The leader, West, after East's double of six spades, should lead a diamond.

Basically, in most doubles of slam contracts, the signal given is for the purpose of **ruffing**. Ruffing is the trumping of a suit that a player is void in. Thus, in the previous example, East probably was void in diamonds and could cash an ace in another suit for an immediate setting of the six spade contract.

If the doubler is void in a suit, you might ask, why doesn't he just wait to trump that suit when it is played later? The reason is simple. A declarer who knows what he's about, and seeing that there is going to be unbalanced distribution of suits, will immediately draw trumps when he's in the lead, and thus deplete East's trumps. Without trumps, East will be unable to win the diamond trick.

THE IMMEDIATE CUE BID

Of all the defensive bids available to you, this is the strongest. It is the equivalent of a two-bid and is forcing to game. It promises partner either an ace or a void in the bid suit.

To refresh our recollection, a cue bid is defined as bidding the opener's bid suit. Previously, in the takeout double section, we saw it used as a response to doubler's takeout bid. Now we examine it as an immediate bid instead of in response to a takeout double or overcall. For example, suppose the bidding has gone as follows:

SOUTH	WEST	NORTH	EAST
1 Diamond	2 Diamonds		

The two diamond bid is to be construed as a cue bid, telling partner you have a powerful hand. This bid forces partner to bid to game. His response will be the same as if you bid a takeout double, so review that section for correct responses. The following would be a typical hand calling for a cue bid.

♠ A J 10 4   ♥ A K Q 5   ♦ -   ♣ K Q J 9 8

10. DECLARER'S PLAY

There are several tactical strategies available to the declarer as he attempts to make his contract. The cards he holds, the dummy's cards, the first lead and the previous bidding by both his partnership and the other side are some of the factors he must review to formulate his correct playing strategy.

DECLARER'S STRATEGY

After the bidding is completed and the first play has been made toward dummy, and the dummy exposed, the declarer should take time to plan his strategy for the playing out of the hand.

First he should review the bidding in his mind, and weigh the information it has revealed. If only one defender bid, he must be assumed to have the high-card strength that is missing from both the declarer's and dummy's hands. This isn't always the rule, but is true often enough to be a definite consideration.

Perhaps one of the defenders opened the bidding. If he opened with a major suit, and played five-card majors as a bidding convention, it can be assumed that he holds five cards in that suit, and that his point count in high cards and distributional strength is at least thirteen. With this information, an appropriate strategy can be planned.

If one defender doubled the contract, and there were no other bids entered by the defenders, the declarer would then have to surmise the reason for the double. Perhaps the doubler has the cards to stop the contract, or perhaps he believes that his partner is holding those cards. A penalty double is a red flag shown to the declarer and he must adjust his play accordingly.

If neither defender bid, then there is nothing to be learned from their bidding, other than the fact that both players opposing the contract may not have biddable hands or enough of a point count. If the contract he is playing is at a low-level, such as two or three in a suit, it may be that the honors are evenly distributed between the two defenders, so that they weren't able to make a viable bid. So, even passes by the other side convey information to the declarer.

After the opening lead, the declarer should examine the card led before playing one of dummy's cards. Why that lead? Why that suit? Is it a lead from the player's best suit, or is it a lead that hopes to find high cards in that suit in partner's hand? Is it really the correct lead based on the situation and dummy's strength, or is it the lead of a weak player? Which brings us to another point.

One of the factors that should be examined by the declarer is the relative strength of the players he is up against. Are they good players? Are they experts? Or are they mediocre or weak players. In rubber bridge, after a while, the strength of the players will become apparent. In duplicate bridge, where a steady stream of new partnerships come by to play against your side, you will not be so sure of their qualifications.

To return to the opening lead - once the lead is made, the declarer must then and there ask himself: in what hand does he want to take the trick, if he can win it. If he does take the trick, what will be his next lead? Before answering these questions, declarer must examine the cards in his hand and in dummy's and decide on a strategy.

He should count his absolute winning tricks, then determine what course of play to follow in the event the sure tricks will not be enough to fulfill the contract. Most of the time they won't be enough. He must ask himself which suits are likely to produce other tricks. Will he have to finesse, that is, play a card such as a low card to dummy's A Q holding in the hope that the player to his left holds the king and won't be able to play it? If the finesse succeeds the queen will hold up as an extra won trick.

Or will he try for a ruff, playing a suit from dummy that he is void in, and trumping it? Or should he first draw trumps in case the other side is void in a suit, preventing them from ruffing? If he attacks trumps, will the split be right for him? If there are five trumps out and he holds the A K, will the trumps break perfectly at 3-2 with the queen in the hand holding only two trumps, so that he can establish his other trumps as winners? What will he do if the trump split is 4-1? One guide for him will be the table later on in this section showing the percentages of suit splits.

Here are three basic rules to follow in declarer's play.

THE THREE BASIC RULES OF DECLARER'S STRATEGY

A. First and foremost, declarer should stay alert. He must remember the bids, the leads, the cards discarded during the tricks played. He must also keep track of the suits, and know precisely how many cards in each suit have been played. Without this knowledge, he will severely handicap himself. He cannot afford to play a guessing game, not really knowing how many of a particular suit remains to be played. That is the sign of the mediocre player.

B. He must plan his strategy as soon as possible. He should have some idea of what he will attempt before the first card is led to dummy, but once he sees that card, and dummy's hand is exposed, as mentioned before, he should pause and contemplate his playing strategy. Knowing what to do, he should then follow through. In case of bad breaks in the suits held by defenders, he must plan an alternate strategy, if that is possible, which will enable him to make the contract.

If he finds he will be set, declarer must play to limit the tricks he is set by. At no point during the playing of the hand should he play sloppily or let his mind wander. He must keep track of the cards and suits played and know just how many cards of each suit remain. We cannot emphasize this point enough.

C. Declarer must be aware of and play percentages. He cannot disregard the odds in any situation. If West, an opponent, opened the bidding, he cannot count on East to have all the high cards. If a finesse has only a 50-50 chance of succeeding, while the chance of establishing a long suit are 68% in his favor, he must establish that long suit, and not disregard this favorable opportunity.

Having discussed percentages, it might be a good time to now show the probability of breaks in the suits.

PROBABILITY OF BREAKS IN SUITS

As mentioned before, it may become essential to know the probable division of cards in particular suits held by your opponents, in order to fulfill your contract. Of course, the division won't always adhere to the odds but as a guide to the possible breaks of suits, the table below should be known and if possible, memorized.

Suppose you are declarer and hold five of a suit. The dummy also holds five of the same suit. There are three cards out against you in that suit. How will they break? Looking at the chart below you can readily see that 78% of the time the opponents' holdings will be split 2-1.

All of the percentages listed are approximate.

Number of Cards in Suit Against You	Possible Division of Cards	Percentage
Two	1-1	52%
	2-0	48%
Three	2-1	78%
	3-0	22%
Four	3-1	50%
	2-2	40%
	4-0	10%
Five	3-2	67%
	4-1	29%
	5-0	4%
Six	4-2	48%
	3-3	35%
	5-1	15%
	6-0	2%
Seven	4-3	61%
	5-2	31%
	6-1	7%
	7-0	1%

Let's now examine some of the strategies open to declarer as he plays out his hand.

RUFFING

To refresh our recollection, ruffing is defined as the trumping of a led suit, other than trumps, because you are void in the led suit. Let's look at a simple illustration of this. You are South, the declarer, playing the contract in spades.

```
                    North
                    ♠ 5 4
                    ♥ Q 10
                    ♦ A
                    ♣ 5 2


    West            South            East
                    ♠ J 6 3
                    ♥ K 10
                    ♦ Q 7
                    ♣ -
```

West leads the 3 of clubs, you play the deuce from dummy, and East plays the queen. Being void in clubs, you ruff the trick by trumping with your 3 of spades. Now you can lead the 7 of diamonds from your hand, and win the diamond trick with the ace of diamonds in dummy. Then you lead the remaining club from dummy and again trump it in your hand. Another ruffing trick has been won.

The ability to ruff tricks is a great help to declarer, and that's why valuations are put on singletons and doubletons when adding up the total points of a hand. Of course, this only relates to suit contracts. In no-trump contracts, where ruffing is impossible because there is no trump suit, only honor points are counted when determining the strength of the hand.

CROSSRUFFING

Crossruffing may be defined as a way to take tricks by ruffing in each of the partnership's hands, thus using the trumps available separately. In other words, declarer can lead a suit to dummy, one that dummy is void in, trump it there, then lead one of dummy's suits (other than trump) and trump it in declarer's hand, because declarer is void in that suit. This use of sidesuits to establish ruffing tricks in both hands is a powerful strategy for declarer.

The following is an illustration of successful cross-ruffing. (x = indifferent card, from 2-8)

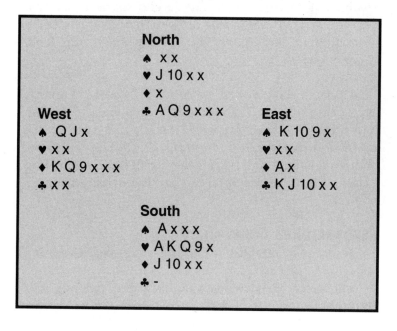

North
♠ x x
♥ J 10 x x
♦ x
♣ A Q 9 x x x

West
♠ Q J x
♥ x x
♦ K Q 9 x x x
♣ x x

East
♠ K 10 9 x
♥ x x
♦ A x
♣ K J 10 x x

South
♠ A x x x
♥ A K Q 9 x
♦ J 10 x x
♣ -

East was dealer. The bidding went

EAST	SOUTH	WEST	NORTH
Pass	1 Heart	Pass	2 Clubs
Pass	2 Hearts	Pass	4 Hearts
Pass	Pass	Pass	

West led the (S) Q, which was won by South's ace. Now, looking over dummy, South saw that his best strategy was to crossruff. To do this he had to get rid of the diamond in dummy's hand, so he led a small diamond, which drove out East's ace.

East, sensing that declarer was interested in ruffing, and seeing the void in dummy's diamond suit, played a small heart, trying to deplete declarer of his hearts as soon as possible. South won the heart trick in his hand, then led a diamond to dummy, ruffing it by playing a trump from dummy's hand.

Declarer then cashed (won the trick with) dummy's ace of clubs, discarding a diamond, then led a small club and ruffed it in his hand. Now he could play another diamond and trump it with dummy's 10, then lead another club from dummy and ruff it in his own hand. Crossruffing back and forth between the two hands, he easily made his contract.

ESTABLISHING LONG SUITS

In order to establish a long suit and take in winning tricks with the small cards in that suit, the declarer must be certain that the defenders cannot trump the long suit. As a precaution, therefore, he should play out trump, exhausting the defenders' trump holdings before running the long suit. Once the defenders are out of trump, they are helpless to stop the declarer from cashing in tricks in the long suit, provided, of course, that they don't have a stopper to win a trick or two of their own in that suit.

The above strategy works for suit contracts. In no-trump contracts, the defenders, acting first by having the first lead, will try and establish their long suit. It often is a race against time to see which side establishes their long suit first. This becomes vitally important, because a declarer doesn't have to worry about trump, and once the other side is depleted of a suit he still has cards in, he can run all his remaining cards for winners.

In no-trump contracts, three factors must be taken into consideration by declarer. He must win with his honor cards, he must establish a long suit, if he has one, so his small cards in that suit can be winners, and if he a bit short of tricks, he must try a finesse or two. Which brings us to another important declarer strategy, the finesse.

THE FINESSE

The finesse may be defined as a lead or play toward a broken sequence of cards, such as A-Q or K-J in order to take advantage of the favorable position of the opponent's card so as to make the trick. The following illustration will make the concept simple. You are South and the declarer. North, the dummy, holds the A Q of diamonds. You play a small diamond toward dummy in the hope of finessing the king, which you believe is held by West.

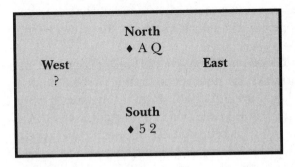

You lead the deuce of diamonds to the A Q. If West holds the king, he is in a bind. If he plays the king, it will fall to the Ace, and then your queen will be a winning trick, being now the highest ranking diamond left unplayed. If he doesn't play the king, you play the queen as a finesse, winning with the queen, and then your ace is boss.

In any event, you will attempt to finesse the queen. No matter what West plays, you'll play the queen, hoping that East doesn't hold the king. If East has the king, your finesse will fail.

Before attempting the finesse, you should review the bidding of the defenders, and review their play up to that point. Did West or East enter the bidding? If West put in a bid, then it's more likely she holds the king. Has East avoided leading a diamond when it was his turn to lead. Perhaps he doesn't want to lead away from his king.

Also, before trying the finesse, you should ask yourself if there is some other way to win the tricks you need. Should you establish your long suit after drawing out trumps? What kind of split in the remaining cards of your long suit should you expect to find in the defenders' hands? Study the percentage table of possible splits. The more you know, the more you can reason out the consequences of your play, the better player you'll be.

ENTRIES

An **entry** is a means of securing the lead in a particular hand. In order to enter the hand, that hand must have a card high enough to win a trick, or be able to trump a lead to it, being void in a suit. Two simple examples. You want to have an entry into dummy's hand. Dummy holds the ace of clubs and you lead a small club from your hand. The ace of clubs is your entry into dummy's hand.

Now you want to enter your hand from a lead by dummy. You are void in hearts (spades are trump). You lead a heart from dummy and trump it in your hand. You've secured an entry into your hand.

There are times when a contract is set because the declarer couldn't secure an entry into one of the hands, either his own or dummy's, in order to cash the winning tricks that were there. For example, let's look at the South and North hands in the following example. South is the declarer, and spades are trumps.

North
♠ -
♥ A K 4
♦ 9 6
♣

South
♠ Q J 7
♥ -
♦ J 10
♣

South desperately needs those two heart tricks in dummy's hand, but he has no way to enter dummy if he is leading from his hand. He has no hearts or clubs, and his diamonds are higher than those held by dummy. This is a good example of a declarer who hasn't thought out his strategy, so as to leave himself with an entry into dummy's hand. He may have played out his minor suits willy-nilly, not realizing that he should have left a higher card in clubs or diamonds in dummy's hand to secure an entry.

A good rule to follow is this; always make sure that you secure entries into both your hands, declarer's and dummy's, when playing out a contract. If you will need an entry later on in the game, plan for it. Don't use up a valuable entry early on by giving up a high card in a hand that will become devoid of entries. Entries are valuable and must be carefully preserved.

11. DEFENDER'S PLAY

When defending against the contract, the first object of the defenders is to defeat the contract. If the contract can't be set, then the next object is to limit the declarer to just enough tricks to make the contract, without allowing him to make overtricks. In rubber bridge, where overtricks are scored above the line, this is somewhat important. In duplicate bridge, where you and all other partnerships in your category (either West-East or North-South) are judged by how well you defend against a particular contract, it is of utmost importance.

When playing duplicate bridge, often the difference between a top score and a mediocre one boils down to an overtrick. If your partnership is defending against a contract, and you allow an overtrick, while all the other partnerships, playing the same cards your side held, limit the other team to just the contract itself, you'll end up with low score. In duplicate bridge, every trick counts; and we suggest, as you become experienced at bridge and have a steady partner, that you hone your skill at duplicate bridge.

The most important defensive play is the opening lead, since the correct lead often ends up setting the contract while the wrong lead allows the declarer to have his way and easily make the contract and possibly one or more overtricks as well. So, let's begin our discussion of the defender's play with a study of opening leads.

OPENING LEADS - CHOOSING THE SUIT

As we know, the defenders lead the first trick, and the lead falls on the player to the left of the declarer, who leads to the dummy. The dummy's cards remain closed till the lead is made; then the dummy's hand is exposed, and dummy no longer is involved in the play of the hand. It is the declarer vs. the two defenders.

The first question the leader must ask himself is this: What suit do I lead? Here is a general guidline to choosing the correct suit.

• If your partner has doubled to indicate his preference for an opening suit, lead that suit.

• Where there has been no double directing a particular lead, lead the suit bid by your partner.

• If your partner hasn't bid, then you can lead your own best suit. But you have to be careful not to lose control of the hand too early if you give away your strength at the beginning. If partner has raised your bid suit, by all means lead it.

• If a suit has gone unbid, it is a good idea to lead that suit, since it might be the weak point of the opponents and your partner may have some high card strength in that particular suit.

If there is more than one unbid suit, calculate from the bidding if the dummy has strength in that suit and lead through the dummy, if possible, rather than to declarer's strength. It is always best to lead through the dummy, that is, to play a card to dummy's strength, rather than to declarer's power. For example, if dummy is holding A Q 9 of a suit, and you lead that suit, you're putting the question right to declarer. Which card should he play?

Should he try for the finesse immediately, by playing the queen? Should he try for a **deep finesse** (where three cards are missing; here the king, jack and 10) and play the 9?

On the other hand, if you lead to declarer's strength, if declarer is holding the A Q 9 of that suit, then you're putting your partner in a bind if he's holding K 10 of that suit.

• If you're unsure of what suit to lead, it is best to lead through dummy's strength, since, as shown above, that gives your partner the perfect position (third) to play his strong cards.

• If you gathered from the bidding that declarer has a long powerful trump suit, avoid leading a trump.

• If you learned from the bidding that the opponents have weak trump, and that the declarer will attempt to make a number of tricks by ruffing or crossruffing, then lead trump to deplete their trumps and prevent this from happening.

• If you hold a singleton, lead it if you suspect that your partner is holding the ace and can immediately win the trick and then play back the same suit for you to ruff.

• If you have good trump holdings (four or more) and a long side suit as well, lead the long suit, forcing declarer to trump. He then weakens his trumps so that at a later time you can establish that long suit.

• Against no-trump contracts, lead your longest and strongest suit, unless an opponent has bid that suit. If your hand is extremely weak, with no suit that looks inviting to lead, try to figure out which suit your partner has some strength in.

CHOOSING A LEAD CARD - SUIT CONTRACTS

The following are standard leads, both in suit and no-trump, acknowledged by expert play.

From any sequence of honors, lead the top card.
1. K Q J or K Q 10 - lead the king.
2. Q J 10 or Q J 9 - lead the queen
3. J 10 9 or J 10 8 - lead the jack.

In this instance, the same rule would apply to leads against no-trump contracts.
• A suit headed by A K - lead the king. If your only holding in the suit is A K - lead the ace.
• A three-card suit headed by A K x or K Q x - lead the king. If the three-card suit is headed by Q J x - lead the queen. With J 10 x - lead the jack.
• In the following instances, if partner has bid a suit and you lead his suit, do the following: With a three-card suit headed by one honor, such as K 8 6 or Q 9 4 - lead the lowest card. However, if your three-card suit is headed by an ace, such as A 9 2, lead the ace.
• A four-card holding, with the top two cards in immediate sequence, such as K Q x x or Q J x x - lead the top card of the holding. When holding the A K x x in a four card holding, lead the ace.
• If the four-card holding is headed by only one honor, such as J x x x or K x x x, lead the lowest card in the holding.
• If holding only a doubleton, lead the top card of your suit. If you have an 8 6 - lead the 8. Holding a 10 9 - lead the 10.

If your partner hasn't made a bid, lead from the following holdings as directed.
• When holding three honors in a four-card sequence, such as Q J 10 6 or K Q 10 4, lead the highest honor.
• When holding a four-card suit with an honor at the top, such as Q x x x or K x x x, lead the lowest card in the suit.

• When holding a three-card suit with the top card be ing an honor, such as K 6 3 or Q 9 2, lead the lowest card of the suit.

• When holding the A K as doubleton, lead the ace.

• Holding a doubleton such as 10 9 or 9 8, lead the top card of the two-card sequence.

• Note - If you hold any sequence of three cards with an A Q at the top, such as A Q x, A Q J or A Q 10, do not lead this suit. You are depriving yourself of making both the A and Q as winning tricks by leading away from this holding.

LEADS AGAINST NO-TRUMP CONTRACTS

In no-trump contracts, subject to the following exceptions, when you have the lead, experts advice playing the fourth-highest card from your longest and strongest suit. There is a reason for this advice.

These are the exceptions to the above rule. When your partner has made an overcall or bid a suit during the bidding and you hold two or three small cards in that suit, play the top card you hold. That is, unless you hold an honor heading a three-card suit (in partner's suit) . In that case you'd lead the small card. But if you hold an honor in a doubleton, lead the honor.

When your partner hasn't bid, but dummy bid a suit without a response in that same suit by declarer, you should lead that suit through dummy's strength in the hope of finding your partner with strength in that suit.

If your partner doubled the no-trump contract (especially three no-trump) and neither of you has bid, lead the dummy's first bid suit. This is a conventional lead through dummy's strength.

The following are conventional leads against no-trump contracts when your partner has bid.
- If holding A x x x or K x x x, lead the fourth best card.
- If holding K x x, Q x x or J x x, lead the third best or lowest card.
- If holding A x, K J, Q J or 9 8 (8 7, 7 6, etc.), lead the top card.

If your team has made no bids and dummy has bid, play dummy's suit.
- If holding Q J 10 x x or A K Q x x x - lead the top cards from these suits.
- If holding A x x x, K Q J x, K x x x or Q x x x, lead fourth best.
- If holding 10 x, play the 10. With J 10, lead the jack. If your holding is a three-card suit such as 9 7 5, play the 9.

OTHER DEFENSIVE PLAYS

After the opening lead has been made, you, as defender, can now study the dummy, to see what it reveals. You should pause here, just as you would if you were the declarer, to study your strategical goals. Probably you'll have time to think things out, because the declarer is seeing the dummy for the first time and making his own plans. At this point, from the bidding and from your partner's lead, you should have quite a bit of information.

In addition to this information, we're going to set forth general guidelines for defensive play that you should study carefully.

SECOND HAND LOW

As a general rule, the second hand plays a low card. When a card is led on any trick, the next player to act is the second hand, and he should play low. This tactic is a standard one, used to prevent the opponents from running or establishing a suit. Let's see an example of this. South is the declarer and has the lead. You sit West and the dummy is North. You hold A 8 3 of a suit. The declarer leads a 6 of this suit, and you look at dummy's hand. It holds the K Q 5 2 of the suit.

If you put down your ace, you will give up control of the suit, for then dummy's king and queen will be the highest ranking cards of that suit. However, if you play low, putting down the 3, dummy must play either the queen or king, still giving you control of the suit with your ace. If dummy ducks with the 5 or 2, your partner could win the trick with a 9.

Suppose, in the same situation, dummy held the K J 5 2 of the suit. By playing low, you're forcing declarer to make a tough decision. If both the ace and queen is out against him, he might play the king, hoping to force out the ace. You still retain control of the suit with your ace, and now, your partner's queen will be a potential winning trick.

Let's assume that you hold the same cards of the suit, A 8 3, and dummy is holding K 5 3 2. In this instance declarer is holding the queen. If you are second to play, and a 6 is led to you, it still pays to play low. By not playing the ace, you're keeping control of the suit.

Of course, there are exceptions to this and every other defensive rule, but if you play low on second hand, nine times out of ten you're making the right decision.

THIRD HAND HIGH

Playing third hand high is another general rule that will prove correct most of the time. When you are third to play you must endeavor to play high, either to take the trick or to force out higher cards in the fourth hand, which is your opponent's. In the next diagram, you are East. South is the declarer and North the dummy. Your partner, West, is on the lead.

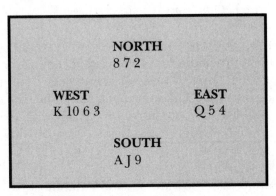

NORTH
8 7 2

WEST
K 10 6 3

EAST
Q 5 4

SOUTH
A J 9

West leads the 3, dummy plays the 2 and now you put on the queen, playing third hand high. If you had played the 5 or 4, South would have won the trick with his 9, and would still retain control of the suit with his ace. By playing the queen, you are either forcing out South's ace or winning the trick. This is an elementary example of the effectiveness of playing third hand high.

COVERING AN HONOR WITH AN HONOR

As a general rule, you should cover an honor with an honor. By this we mean, with a higher honor. By doing this you will either win the trick or force out two of the opponent's honors in one play. However, each situation is different in bridge, and it is not as good a guideline as second hand low or third hand high.

In fact, it may contradict one of these adages. For example, suppose you are West and hold K J 10. Dummy shows A 5 2. South, the declarer, leads a queen. What do you do, play second low or put an honor on an honor?

```
                    NORTH
                     A 5 2
        WEST
        K J 10
```

The correct play is to put an honor on an honor. South's queen is covered by your king. If dummy (North) puts on the ace, your jack and 10 are winning tricks.

Here's another example:

```
                    NORTH (DUMMY)
                    J 10 4
        WEST                        EAST
        Q 8 7 2                     K 9 5

                    SOUTH
                    A 6 3
```

The jack is led from dummy. If East covers with his king, then South would win two tricks in the suit.

East should play low, for if he covers with the king, South will win with his ace; then a return of the 3 will allow West to win with his queen. But this would establish dummy's 10 as a winning second trick. The difference of one trick in this situation may very well decide if the contract will be made or set.

MORE DEFENSIVE PLAYS

When your partner leads a suit at his earliest opportunity, he is usually telling you to return the suit when you're on the lead. This is an important concept in defending against no-trump contracts.

The one hand that will be always be open for your perusal during the course of play is dummy's. We already mentioned how vital it is to lead through dummy's strength. If you see that dummy is holding a suit led by K J or A Q, the missing honor may very well be in your partner's hand. Therefore, if you play that suit through dummy, it may very well be to your side's advantage.

If the dummy is weak, showing no honors, and something like 8 6 5 3 in a suit, and you are to dummy's left, lead up to the weakness of dummy, by playing through declarer's strength. This will put your partner in an advantageous position, enabling him to take in tricks over declarer's cards.

SIGNALS

Since bridge is a partnership game, signals are of utmost importance. Of course, we're referring to legitimate signals which are expressed through the play of the cards. In previous sections on bidding, we've shown how bids can be used as signals for opening leads, and opening leads used to signal partner to play back a particular suit.

One of the best playing signals is the high-low signal.

HIGH-LOW SIGNAL

When your partner plays high-low, he is telling you to continue the suit you've led. If he's holding a suit like K 8 6 3, he'd first drop the 8 on your led suit and then the 3. This is a high-low signal to continue with the same suit.

Sometimes you won't have the luxury of playing an 8 and then the 3. You might have the following cards in a suit: K 6 5 3. In that case, first play the 6 and then play the 3 the next time that suit is led.

When you play a 6 or higher card on partner's led suit, it should alert him to the possibility of a high-low signal. What he must do is examine his hand and the dummy's hand, determining whether a number of small cards are still out. For example, suppose you play the 6 on partner's led suit, and he sees that he holds the 5 4 of that suit, while the dummy is holding the 3 2. He knows the 6 cannot be the start of a high-low signal, since it must be your lowest card in that suit.

In that case, you'd be discouraging him from continuing in the same suit. However, if the 3 was missing from both dummy's and his hand, and he's alert enough, he may now consider that you hold the missing 3, and the 6 you played was a high-low signal, with the 3 coming next from your hand.

Therefore, if you have the luxury of playing a middling card such as a 10, 9 or 8, use them for the signal rather than a lower card which might fool your partner into thinking that you're discouraging the continuation of his led suit.

In defending against suit contracts, any high card played by a partner, followed by a low card of the same suit on the next lead, asks his partner for a continuation of the same suit. This signal usually shows a high honor card, capable of winning the next lead, or shows a void in the suit, allowing a ruff to win the trick.

In no-trump contracts, using the high-low signal can establish a long suit, with small cards in that suit winning a bunch of tricks.

Suppose, in a no-trump contract, your partner opens with the lead of a queen, and dummy shows 5 3 of that suit. You are holding the K 9 6 4. You would signal with the 9, telling your partner to go ahead and continue the suit.

If the queen winds up winning the trick, it is because the declarer held up his ace. The lead of the queen by your partner could have been from a sequence such as Q J 10 x or Q J 8 x. Seeing your high card played, your partner now continues with the suit, playing the jack and this time you play your 2, a definite high-low signal. Declarer will either have to play the ace, losing control of the suit, or lose another trick. Now, if the suit is led again by your partner, your side's small cards will end up as winning tricks.

This signal has another purpose in no-trump contracts, showing your partner the rank of another suit in the dummy's hand, that you'd prefer he play.

Let's suppose that your partner leads an ace towards dummy's hand and you follow with a high card of that same suit. This signal asks your partner to play to the highest ranking of dummy's suits. If dummy still has all four suits in his hand, then a spade lead by your partner would be in order. If dummy was depleted of spades, then a heart lead would be called for.

The high-low signal is also known as an **echo.** When played in a trump suit, it is known as a **trump echo.**

TRUMP ECHO

This is also known as a **trump signal.** This play indicates that the signaller holds exactly three trumps in his hand, and is done when the third trump can be used to ruff a trick.

When a trump is led (by any player), the defender plays an intermediate card, followed by a lower card in the trump suit on the next lead of trumps. For example, if a defender holds a 10 6 4 of trumps, he will first play the 6. On the next trump trick, he will play the 4.

This signal becomes important when a defender has the ability to trump a suit of which he is void. Therefore, when the signaller's partner gets the lead, he should try to ascertain which suit his partner is void in and lead it. By seeing the trump echo, he must assume that his partner is void in one of the side suits, and will trump the correct lead.

This completes our discussion of the essentials of winning bridge, including the scoring, bidding and play of the hands. Study what has been presented and try to play as often as you can. We know you'll enjoy one of the greatest games ever invented. Take your time in learning the correct principles of bidding and play, and you'll end up a winner at bridge. We'll now switch to an anecdote about a bridge rogue, irregularities under the laws of contract bridge, and a final section dealing with duplicate bridge.

12. A ROGUE AT BRIDGE: MR. C'S STORY

We'll call the person about to be described Mr. C. (C standing for cheat). He was an excellent player, a potential champion who occasionally liked to play in the more important duplicate tournaments. He had a steady partner, his wife, but he played with her only in rubber games. She was almost as good as he was, and could cheat just as effectively, but in a duplicate tournament out of town (he was a New Yorker) what could be better than mixing master points with pleasure? And his pleasure was young girls or young women (his bridge pupils or acquaintances), who would take the trip with him, stay at the same hotel, and have the honor of being his partner.

It was quite an honor, because to play with him was an experience. It was having as one's partner the perfect player. He made no wrong bids; he made no wrong plays; he could gauge all the hands immediately by the bidding. He would gently guide your play by correct leads, by legitimate signals. I played with him in a couple of small duplicate games in Manhattan and I didn't even have to bid to get to the correct contract. He had that instinct that I've never seen in any other player. His name is not a household word - far from it - but in big rubber games he is a demon, and those who have faced him for large stakes will never forget him.

Mr. C is getting old, but age has not taken away any of his sharpness. Now he still has pretty girls around him (his pupils, not acquaintances), but they're near him for his charm alone. Alas, age has withered him that way. They still love to play bridge with him as a partner, and they love to listen to his anecdotes about the great players and the great and not-so-great hands he has held, and he has held a lot of them over the years.

He still plays, but not for big stakes anymore. A recent cataract operation has put him at a disadvantage and his eyes can't take the pressure of looking at the cards for too long. But for short intervals of play, he is still a master.

Mr. C, in his prime (and way past his prime as well, if you want to know the truth), would take a pretty girl with him to Chicago, Atlantic City, Los Angeles, wherever a big tournament was being held. There she would be, this young bridge buff, among the great names of the game, all of whom knew Mr. C, by sight or by reputation, and she would be introduced to this great player and that one. The men introduced were courtly and getting on in years, and bridge players of this caliber, away from the table, can be quite gallant.

The girl with Mr. C was an acquiescent cheat. What that means is that she would do whatever Mr. C told her to do. She would obey no matter what her holdings and no matter what her own inclinations. She trusted his ability to handle the game for both of them.

Mr C's advice to her was, "don't do anything on your own. If you have thirteen points, open the bidding with your best suit. Open it, and then shut up. If you have sixteen to eighteen points and are the first bidder, open one no-trump. If you have more than eighteen points, open at a two level with your best suit. If I open the bidding and you have more than six points, bid one over one, and that's it. If you have opening strength after my opening bid, jump and shift to your best suit. In other words, if I bid one heart and you have opening strength, bid two spades, if spades is your suit; and three if your suit is a minor.

"Don't bid otherwise. Don't bid after your opening bid or your response. If I bid four no-trump, bid your aces in the Blackwood convention. No other bids. The best bid you can make is to shut your mouth. After your one bid, I'll handle it.

"If I lead a small card or play a small card and you get in, lead a minor suit; which one should be apparent to you. If you don't know which one, lead one of them but not a major suit. If I play a high card, lead a major suit. If I double a slam and bid a suit, lead that suit. If I double a no-trump and bid a suit, lead that suit. I don't care what you're holding, do as I say."

And there would be the girls, playing with this magician. They did very well, winning a couple of trophies, winning master points, even winning a tournament. He had one big advantage - he wasn't married to any of them. Imagine trying to tell a wife, "Don't do anything but shut up. Play and bid only as I direct."

I asked Mr. C how this could work against really good players.

"It worked best against the best players, believe it or not. Let me give you an example. My girl of the moment and myself sit down in a duplicate tournament against a husband-and-wife team, both good players. Both may or may not know me well, but they don't know the girl, haven't seen her around. Just watching her pick up the cards they know she's hardly ever touched a deck of cards in her life. Maybe I just taught her the game a couple of months before. But she follows instructions.

"They look at the conventions I put on the sheet. I show Blackwood. They ask me if I play Stayman. Worse, they ask my girl. She gives them a blank look. She knows as much about Stayman as I know about brain surgery. No, I say, we don't play Stayman.

"After this short exchange, they know she's a yokel, and they're already licking their chops. A good high score, they figure, against this pair. Here's old Mr. C with a dumb chick he had to take along, else how can he get away from the missus? That's their first two mistakes. First, I can get away from my wife any damn time I please. And second, they're getting overconfident. We pick up our cards and the bidding begins. I'm sitting West, and South opens with a pass. I look at my cards and have an opening bid, maybe twelve points in high cards, but with my partner I've got to get into the bidding. I bid any suit; it doesn't matter to me. I bid one club. I want to see what my partner has. I may not even have a club, but it's a low bid, and if my partner responds, we keep the bidding low.

"Right away the wife, who's about to bid, looks at the sheet to see if I put down artificial club or five-card majors or whatever. All it says is Blackwood. She looks at her hand, this witch, and bids one spade. An overcall. I know she can't be strong enough to double then, and now I wait for my partner to bid. She knows nothing about overcalls or doubles; she only knows what I told her. She's still busy counting her points and says two hearts.

"Now the husband has his turn. I know we have at least eighteen points in our hands, and they have at best twenty-two, so where's the contract going? Nowhere. He bids two spades, and I look over my hand. I got a singleton club, a few hearts, a few spades, and a strong diamond suit. I say three clubs.

"The wife doubles right away. My partner passes. She has no other choice because my instructions were to keep quiet after her one bid. The husband passes, and I bid three diamonds. Wifey doubles, and all pass, and there I am in three diamonds.

The hand was cold. My partner gave me seven points and three diamonds headed by the jack. I had six of my own headed by the ace king. Of course, our method of bidding threw them off, but they were too confident to begin with.

The husband and wife were stunned. Far from getting top score, they were screwed up by the deal. They started arguing with me, asking how I could bid one club with a diamond opening bid, but as nature took its course, they started arguing with each other."

"Why didn't you shift to clubs?" the husband wanted to know, and "Why should I?" the wife replied, "it would have made no difference." And then they started arguing about the bids, and how could she double three diamonds. "Why not?" she angrily replied, and so on and so forth. Meanwhile, we had moved to another table. My beautiful girl friend sat down, kept her mouth shut, and we came off with another nice score."

I asked Mr. C about other duplicate-bridge games which didn't involve pretty girls.

"I sometimes was paid by my pupils to enter duplicate tournaments with them. Some of them were fairly well off and would pay all my expenses, wherever it was. And of course they were sports in other ways. If they wanted a good partner, I played that way, perfectly legit. They enjoyed it; I didn't, but got a good weekend out of it, so it was fun anyway. Others were desperate for master points and they figured I was the perfect vehicle to get them, so off we would go. If they were very, very bad, I gave them the same pep talk I gave the cuties.

"Sometimes they were fairly good and wanted all the edge. If the players we were sitting down with were very strong, I would tell the partner, "Sit up and pay attention this hand." If the players were poor, I would say, "Sit down and play well this time."

"Sometimes I would show them little hand signals to indicate my card strength or a lead. If I touched the right-hand part of the deck, it was spades; the extreme left was clubs; near the spades was hearts; and near the clubs was diamonds. Simple and easy. These partners were always perfect leaders.

"Just holding the cards up a little was a strong hand, and down, a weak hand. Sometimes I would hold the cards up and pass, and my partner knew I was ready to spring a trap. Things like that. I could go on and on, because, in a partnership game, with words and gestures and lighting of cigarettes and touching of glasses, my God, it's like being a coach at third base."

Mr. C told me about some rubber games he was involved in.

"I always played for high stakes, because what was the

use otherwise? I would get sick of sitting on my ass and playing cards sometimes, and it was no fun playing a couple of dumb suckers and winning a couple of bucks. I'd rather be at the trotters, or trying to work my way into some girl's pants. But if the money was right, there I was. How did I do it?

"My wife, God rest her soul, was a great bridge player and a great, I hesitate to use the word "cheat." Let me just say she could play with the best of them. If I could, I'd play with her against a couple of suckers. It was better sometimes to play with a stranger, because if they knew my wife was playing and we were the only winners, even though we switched partners they would get suspicious.

"I had several partners, all topnotch players. In bridge, the game is so technical and skillful that if you're a cheat but not a good player, you might still be at a disadvantage. So I had a few good partners. We would be at some club where there were big games, and we'd take on two suckers - either they were strangers or they knew each other - and we'd play a rubber game for some big money. Of course, to the suckers, I didn't know my partner, and we'd play as partners or switch; it didn't matter.

"Either way, the suckers got it. If I had a sucker as a partner, sometimes with a big hand I'd pass, then throw them in if all passed. Sometimes I'd let the sucker win. Most of the time I'd try and be dummy and let the sucker play - a sure way for him to lose.

"The ideal game is to have only one sucker and three sharps in the game. That's the perfect setup, and here's how it's done. We could play at a club or, better still, in some hotel room we rented in one of the better hotels. We'd never use marked cards - they have little value in bridge - but we'd keep a stacked deck sometimes.

"In cheating, there are two things to remember. One, if the sucker has a little larceny, he's ideal for a cheat. Two, if he has to persuade you to play with him, it's an ideal situation. So, all of us strangers to each other perhaps, but known only as good card players, we'd set the sucker up. One of us would bring him along to watch - only watch. There'd be four of us, and since we would tell him we were all great players, he could only watch.

"Watching bridge is like watching someone get laid. You want to get into the act. Here we'd play a couple of rubbers in this hotel suite, with the sucker looking on, just drooling. Then one of the foursome would have to leave, and I'd say, "Let's call it a night." But the sucker would say, "Wait a minute, why not me?"

"I was always the good guy. I'd say, "No, it's a big game, and you're not up to it. You're really not. I didn't invite you up to lose your money."

"Well, to a sucker's honor, the idea that he's not that good really hurts. He insists that he is up to us in skill, and so, reluctantly, we let him in. We often played steady partners or, better still, rotated. We'd rotate, telling the sucker we wanted to even things out.

"If you really put a sucker down as to his skill, he gets stubborn. He wants to play with only one partner. So we let him. After a few bad rubbers, in which we murder them, my partner and I leave the room. We go for a drink, or water, or a cigarette, and we leave the sucker with his part-ner, who tells him, "Look, buddy, I'm losing a fortune. Why don't you pick another partner?" The sucker protests, then the partner says, "Okay, play with me, but we need a little help. Now here's what we do."

"As he explains his cheating methods, nine times out of ten, or ninety-nine times out of a hundred, the sucker is all ears. He wants to win, and so just a little larceny won't hurt anybody. And if he agrees, he's going to be doubly murdered. If he backs out, the partner says, "Never mind. Take another partner. Take Mr. C, the good guy." And so now I inherit the honest sucker. It still does him no good.

"But if he goes along with the partner's suggestion about cheating, he is buried. We don't even let him win twenty percent of the time, and we can even get a little reckless because he has no protest - he's a cheat himself."

I asked Mr. C about any advice he could give.

"Play in a legitimate bridge club, or among friends at home, and play for the love of the game. It's a great game, a skillful game, and the mere skill involved in this game should supply all the excitement you'd ever want."

13. IRREGULARITIES IN BRIDGE

The following are the most common irregularities in bridge; not all of the possible infractions of the rules can be listed here. The reader is advised to read the *Laws of Contract Bridge*, published by the American Contract Bridge League.

FAILURE TO FOLLOW SUIT

If a player has failed to follow suit - that is, failed to play the same suit as led when he still holds a card of that suit - this is called a **revoke**, and any player may call attention to the failure and demand that the revoke be corrected. A revoke is established if the trick is finished and the revoking player plays another card.

The offending player may correct his revoke without penalty, but this must be done before the trick is completed, which occurs when a new lead is played.

If a revoke is established, the penalty is two tricks. If, however, after the revoke occurs the revoking side does not make any more tricks, then the penalty is just the one revoked trick.

EXPOSED CARDS

Any card dropped on the table face up becomes an exposed card and must be left on the table. If the lead is in the same suit, that card must remain on the table and be played.

If another suit is led and the player whose card is exposed is void in that suit, then the card exposed must be played to the lead.

If the lead is to a suit other than the exposed card's suit, the offender must play the correct suit, but must lead the exposed card if he subsequently gets the lead or play it at the first opportunity.

LEAD OUT OF TURN

If it is one defender's turn to lead, but the other defender leads instead, the declarer may accept the lead, or demand that the correct defender play the same suit or play any other suit but that suit. The incorrect leader then returns the card to his hand.

DECLARER LEADING OUT OF TURN

Should the declarer lead from his hand instead of from the dummy when it is the dummy's turn to lead, he may replace the card in his hand, provided no other card was played by the defenders, and then lead a card of the same suit from dummy. He does not have to play the card incorrectly led, but must merely follow suit. Should the dummy be void in the incorrect suit led form his hand, any card may be led from dummy.

LEAD BEFORE THE AUCTION IS COMPLETED

If a player makes a lead before the bidding is completed, the offender must leave the card face up on the table until the auction is completed. If the card led is an honor (jack, queen, king, or ace), then the offender's partner is barred from the bidding during the auction.

Should the card led be lower than an honor, it becomes an exposed card and is left face up on the table. If the auction is bought by the opposing team, the declarer can accept that card as lead, or ask for the offender's partner to lead that suit. He may also ask for a different lead. Should he do this, the offender may replace the exposed card in his hand.

PASS OUT OF TURN DURING THE AUCTION

Any player making a pass out of turn must pass when it is his turn to bid on the next round of bidding.

BID OUT OF TURN

Any player making a bid out of turn (other than a pass) bars his partner from making any bids until the entire auction is over. The offender, however, is not barred and may continue to bid if he desires.

INSUFFICIENT BID

When a player makes a bid, or response, or overcall lower than the preceding bid of the opponents, he must make the correct bid of the same suit at a higher level. Should he decide not to, but instead bids another suit, his partner is barred from any bids for the entire auction.

CLAIMING ALL TRICKS

When a declarer, during the play of the cards, claims the balance of the tricks, he must announce the manner in which he intends to play his cards out, and then must lay his entire hand, face up, on the table.

If he claims all tricks and does not announce the manner in which he intends to play out the hand, he must play all his top honor cards and take no finesses, unless the finesse was established on a previous play.

14. DUPLICATE BRIDGE

INTRODUCTION

Because rubber bridge is dependent upon the luck of the deal, duplicate bridge was devised to eliminate this element of chance. In duplicate bridge, identical hands are played by all participants, which usually consist of eight or more partnerships. In order for this to be done, each partnership plays either as a North-South team or as an East-West team, and each participant plays the identical hands held by the previous players sitting, for example, as North, if he is North. Thus the relative skill of the players manifests itself without the luck of the deal.

This device holds four hands of a deal. The standard board is usually of metal. On it is an arrow pointing to the North hand. One of the sections designates the dealer, who is the first to bid. Also the vulnerability of any particular team is marked.

One of the advantages of playing duplicate bridge is that a player cannot afford either to bid or play sloppily since each deal is of the same importance as every other deal. Therefore, defending a one-diamond contract has as much validity as defending seven no-trump. It may yield more points to the defenders, since there is more likelihood that the seven-no-trump contract will be a cold, laydown hand, whereas the one-diamond contract might possibly be a mismatch.

MECHANICS OF PLAY

Each partnership is designated as either a North-South or East-West team, and is assigned a table and number at the outset of play. There will be a duplicate board at the table, with a deck of cards divided into four parts. The cards are put together, shuffled, and dealt out at random, thirteen cards to each player. Once each player get his thirteen cards, he plays these cards, and all subsequent players at the same position during the session play the same cards.

In order to retain the same cards, when a trick is played the card played is not put into the center of the table but is put face up in front of the player, and then turned over after the play. If the trick was won, the longer edges face the partnership. After the play of the entire hand, the cards are picked up by each player and put into the slot marked for the player. The North player puts his cards into the North slot, etc. Then one team (East-West, for example) remains at the table, while the North-South team moves to other tables to play against other East-West teams.

SCORING

In duplicate bridge, there are no rubbers to be made. Each game played is a separate entity. If a contract below game is made, there is a premium of fifty points in addition to the actual points. This is so whether or not the partnership is vulnerable. Making game when vulnerable is an additional bonus of 500 points; when not vulnerable, it is 300 additional points.

To facilitate the scoring, a scoresheet is given to each team. On it is mentioned the *board number* (each board has one), the *pair number* (each partnership is given one), the *final contract, whom it was played by,* and the *final plus or minus score* and who scored it. After the scores are all in, the team scoring the highest or best score for one side gets the highest total. For example, if there are eight tables, the highest score will be seven (beating the other seven pairs), and so on. The highest total score of a partnership makes that partnership the winner.

The scoresheet is usually folded and kept with the board; it doesn't travel with the pairs. At the end of the game it is collected by the director of the tournament, and then the scores of all the pairs are totaled.

LAWS AND RULES

The laws governing duplicate bridge are put out by the National Laws Commission of the American Contract Bridge League and should be consulted.

American Contract Bridge League
2990 Airways Boulevard, Memphis, TN 38116-3847
(1- 800)264-8786

A FINAL WORD

For those players who have mastered bridge and wish to test their skill at higher levels, duplicate bridge is highly recommended. It is an exciting, competitive game, and through its competitiveness, the player with an open mind can only learn to play even better. It is best to have a steady partner to enjoy the game at its fullest.

15. GLOSSARY

Above The Line - The place on the scoresheet where premium points, honors, overtricks and undertricks are scored.

Auction - The period during which the bidding takes place.

Below The Line - The place on the scoresheet where trick scores are entered.

Bid - A statement during the auction naming a suit, no trump, or a double or redouble, as well as a pass.

Biddable Suit - A holding that meets the minimum requirement for a bid.

Book - The first six tricks taken by the declarer.

Contract - The final bid, with an obligation to win a certain number of tricks.

Dealer - The player who shuffles and deals out the cards.

Declarer - The player who plays out the hand for the partnership that won the bid.

Defenders - The players who play against the declarer.

Doubleton - An original holding of two cards in a suit.

Dummy - The declarer's partner, or the exposed hand of declarer's partner.

Duplicate Board - A device for holding the four separate hands of the players.

Finesse - An attempt to win a trick with a card that is lower than one held by the opponents in the same suit.

Forcing Bid - A bid that forces his partner to keep the auction open.

Game - The fulfillment of the contract sufficient to close out a game.

Grand Slam - The bidding and making of all thirteen tricks by the declarer.

Honors - The five highest trumps or the four aces in no-trump.

Jump Bid - A forcing bid of two or three over a bid suit.

Lead - A card played by the winner of the previous round of play.

Long Suit - The holding of more than four cards in a suit; the longest holding in any suit in a hand.

Major Suit - Spades and hearts.

Minor Suit - Clubs and diamonds.

No Trump - A bid to play out the hand without a trump suit.

Not Vulnerable - A description of a team that hasn't won a game towards rubber.

Opening Bid - The first bid of a suit or no-trump.

Opening Lead - The first card led to the dummy.

Overtrick - A trick won by a declarer in excess of his contract.

Part Score - A trick score total that is less than game.

Penalty Double - A bid which attempts to penalize the opponents for making an incorrect bid.

Point Count - The total of high-card points and distributional points held by a player.

Preemptive Bid - A high opening bid made to shut out the competition.

Rebid - A second bid made by a player in the same suit or no trump.

Redouble - A bid made by the doubled bidder or his partner, increasing the penalties or the trick values in the event the doubled bid becomes the contract.

Response - A bid made in reply to a bid by one's partner.

Responder - The player making a bid in reply to a bid by his or her partner.

Rubber - The winning of two games at rubber bridge by one team.

Set - To defeat the contract.

Signal - A legal method of giving a partner information either by a bid or playing of a card.

Small Slam - The bidding and winning of 12 tricks by the declarer.

Squeeze Play - An end play which forces the opponents to make adverse discards.

Stopper - A card which stops the running of a suit by the opponents.

Suits - Any of the four sets of cards in a pack called spades, hearts, diamonds and clubs.

Takeout Double - A double informing one's partner that the bidder has opening strength, or giving other information about the bidder's hand.

Trick - The taking of cards in a round of play either by high card of the suit or by a trump.

Trump - The suit bid by the winner of the auction.

Void - The holding of no cards of a particular suit.

Vulnerable - The side that has won one game towards a rubber.

X - A symbol representing an indifferent low card of a suit. - Example: A Q J x.

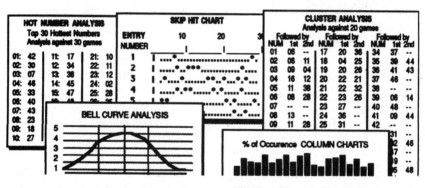